A SONG FOR CRICKET

A SONG FOR CRICKET

David Rayvern Allen

PELHAM BOOKS
LONDON

Dedicated to
David Frith
who has always provided
the inspirational word

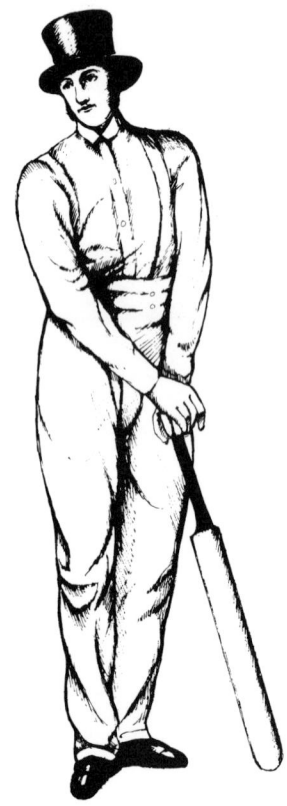

First published in Great Britain by
Pelham Books Ltd
44 Bedford Square
London WC1B 3DU
1981

© 1981 by David Rayvern Allen

All Rights Reserved. No part of this
publication may be reproduced,
stored in a retrieval system, or
transmitted, in any form or by any
means, electronic, mechanical,
photocopying, recording or otherwise, without the prior permission
of the Copyright owner.

Allen, David Rayvern
   A song for cricket.
    1. Songs, English
    2. Cricket
    I. Title
   784.6'8796358   M1740
ISBN 0 7207 1287 4

Typeset in Great Britain
Printed and bound in Singapore

Contents

Acknowledgements	6
Foreword by Tim Rice	7
A Song for Cricket	9
Appendix	188
Credits	209
Index	211
Index of First Lines	218

Acknowledgements

For their invaluable help in the complilation of this book, I am deeply indebted to:

Fritz Spiegl, Benny Green, David Frith, Leslie Gutteridge, Imogen Holst, Bill Sullivan, John Parkinson, Valerie Cummings at the British Library, Peter Wynne Thomas; Jim Coldham. E K (Ted) Brown, Will Rosser at BBC Television Music Library; Tony Barker, John McKenzie, Tony Winder, John Arlott, Tim Rice, Roger Mann, Stephen Green, Anthony Baer, Ian Johnson, Graham Hatton, Patrick Mullins, H (Ossie) Osborne, Marjorie Martineau, The Maharaja of Porbandar, Ian Keith, Philip Cartledge, John Goulstone, the late Cole Lesley, the Noel Coward Estate, E Rotan (Tanny) Sargent, Robert Brooke, Richard Stilgoe, Jonathan Adams, Bruce Ogston, Peter Christie and Instant Sunshine, The Yetties, Bonny Sartin, Perceval Graves, the staff of the BBC Music Library and Popular Music Library, Stephen Best (Nottingham County Library), Peter Wynne-Thomas, Denys Parsons, The Bodleian Library. There are many more who should be included likewise, and months later they are unfortunate victims of my inability to drag actual names from the recesses of my befuddled brain. From them I would beg forgiveness, my appreciation was and is just as strongly felt.

Foreword

It is common knowledge that of all sports cricket boasts the greatest literature, in both quality and quantity. For centuries many of the most distinguished writers of the English language have used their skills to describe the great game. In recent years, although cricket itself has sometimes had to struggle (by and large successfully, I am glad to say) to keep pace with the outrageous demands of the frantic tempo of late twentieth century life, the flow of books and other publications about cricket and cricketers has never been stronger or faster.

The only trouble is that far too many of these works are about the same thing. Every Test series, every tour these days inspires about a dozen books, and it is hard for the cricket lover to work up a colossal enthusiasm for 'The Ashes Regained' when he has already waded through 'Struggle for the Ashes,' 'The Ashes Come Home', 'Return of the Ashes' and 'The Ashes Lost' (this last one presumably written from the point of view of the other side) to name but a selection of the volumes at his disposal a mere few months after the Ashes have come home (or not, if you are on the other side). It hardly matters how gifted the author might be – even Shakespeare would have trouble hitting the best-sellers with 'A Winter's Tale – The Ashes Regained' or 'Love's Labours and the Ashes Lost' if he was eleventh into the market place after Christopher Martin-Jenkins, Henry Blofeld, Jack Fingleton and eight others.

Thus a book like this one is doubly welcome. Not only is it about cricket, it is an original book about cricket. To the best of my knowledge (and to the best of his) David Rayvern Allen's probe into the history of cricket songs is a unique piece of research. By analysis of cricket songs, by the telling of the stories behind the songs, and by the reproduction of many of the greatest cricket lyrics, David has made an important new contribution to the history of the game itself – in a scholarly but also very amusing way.

I have achieved a certain amount of third division notoriety as a lyric writer and have also become well-known as a cricket fanatic. In fact, I sometimes worry about the fact that I am currently more successful as a cricket-lover than as a songwriter. Despite my almost total lack of ability when let loose on a cricket field, I seem to be offered more work in connection with cricket than anything else. (David Rayvern Allen himself is a powerful man at the BBC but despite my leaden hints that I am a man of many parts he has to date only employed me on cricket programmes, but I digress.)

I was about to say that because of my reputation in the above two walks of life it is not surprising that I am often asked if I have any plans to write a musical or even a song about cricket. So far I have resisted the temptation. This is partly because my partner, Andrew Lloyd Webber (Hampshire), has no interest in cricket whatsoever and partly because I cannot see any musical about cricket having much hope of a long run on Broadway. Even David Bowie, one of the most popular British musicians in America, was this year unable to get very far up the U.S. charts with his British No.1 'Ashes To Ashes'. But Sydney these days is an important theatrical centre, and there must be potential audiences in Amritsar and Antigua. Maybe one day . . .

I may never get around to writing a cricket musical, but having read this book I am determined to write a cricket song soon, if only to give myself the chance of appearing in the second edition of this magnificent work. I would be in excellent company as you will shortly discover. From Purcell to Roy Harper David Rayvern Allen's fascinating tale of cricket and song is delight from first stanza to last and at the end of it I guarantee you will not know who won the Ashes.

TIM RICE
Great Milton, December 1980

A Song for Cricket

'What are you doing at the moment?' they ask, no doubt expecting a reply safely couched between the *déjà vu* existence of jet travel and dole queue.

'Looking for cricket songs,' I reply, somewhat self-consciously at having revealed so immediately a bent for ephemeral escapism.

'Cricket songs!' Raised voice, widened eyes, and a desperate cranking of the subconscious in search of something they feel they ought to have deposited long ago.

'I've heard of rugger songs. . . .'

Cricket songs are as ancient as the game itself, a statement which should not be considered in anyway illuminory, as the same principle of musical longevity could be applied to the most mundane and uninspiring activities known to cave or modern man. Although not ancient, a song such as DOES THE CHEWING-GUM LOSE ITS FLAVOUR ON THE BEDPOST OVERNIGHT provides a good example. The habit of reliving and colouring human experience in words and music is a form of emotional expression that helps keep a perspective. A song about the robotic factory conveyor belt or another about advanced Russellian philosophy would make both seem less forbidding and more approachable. Not, one hastens to add, that there are many songs about either.

A lot of the earliest cricket songs must have been lost in the days of illiteracy, when the game's lack of status meant that the few who were equipped to convey to paper the jocular rhymes of the shepherds in the Weald often did not do so. Then later on in the eighteenth and nineteenth centuries there were compositions entitled SONG, which nowadays can mislead, as they had no musical accompaniment. It was a common practice to write short poems in rhymed stanzas in a fairly simple style designed to enhance rather than overshadow the main text. The concentration in this book, however, is on cricket songs that are known, or can reasonably be assumed to have had some music attached, and to record their continuing existence alongside the game they heralded.

Today many of the late nineteenth and early twentieth century songs written for smoking concerts and club dinners seem quaint, trite, jingoistic, and musically banal, and make strange bedfellows with some of the flip offerings of recent years. Yet in each case there is an accurate reflection of the social attitudes, humour and standards prevalent at the time, and if the *lingua franca* has changed, it was just as significant to the people of its age. The cricket song tells its own history, which deserves to be preserved.

The question of whether references to cricket began with the wardrobe accounts of Prince Edward in 1300, we will leave to dusty and didactic custodians of the game's history. The stimulating arguments, no doubt, will continue to rage over whether the easily-led Prince and his notorious playboy companion from Gascony, Piers Gaveston, were indeed the first cricketers known to posterity. Or was it perhaps the youths at play mentioned by Joseph of Exeter in the twelfth century, or maybe it was Audun and Grettir the Strong of Iceland of the eleventh century, or could it possibly, after all, have been the Italian monk in the sixth century? Let us step aside as well from the nettles surrounding cricket's relationship to stoolball. Ye ancient stoolball looks like an immature form of cricket, and is much more likely to have been an elderly and remote cousin rather than a direct forbear. The distance of the relationship, however, does not prevent us mentioning a humorous song sung at Mary the Buxom's Wedding in the play of Don Quixote with music by the leading English composer of the seventeenth century, Henry Purcell: *Come all, great, small, short, tall, away to Stoolball; Down in a Vale on a Summers day, all the Lads and Lasses met to be Merry, a match for Kisses at Stoolball play. . .*, and in case anybody still thinks that rugger songs are the rudest, they ought to know that *Will, Tom, Hall, Dick, and Hugh, Kate, Doll, Sue, Bess, and Moll, with Hodge and Briget* did not stop at kissing.

Purcell gathered his 'Choicest Songs for One, Two, and Three Voices' into two volumes which were published in 1698, nearly three years after his premature death, under the imposing title ORPHEUS BRITANNICUS. The publisher was Henry Playford and he obviously saw the chance of cornering the market, as in that same year he edited and produced the first volume of *Wit and Mirth: Or Pills to Purge Melancholy*. *Pills* has been called the last of the seventeenth-century 'choyce drolleries', and the first of the eighteenth century vocal miscellanies. It contained 'slight' songs of the people — folk and street ballads, coziers catches, pleasant and divertive, which the intellectuals of the day pretended to despise. Mind you, there were a few critics who really did object to the *Pills* on moral grounds, saying that the lewd ditties encouraged 'profaneness and debauchery'.

Pills to Purge Melancholy was later extended into six volumes by the industrious composer and playwright Thomas D'Urfey, and a number of Purcell's songs were incorporated, including COME ALL TO STOOLBALL. D'Urfey presented over eleven hundred songs and poems in the six volumes — a high proportion of which were from his own pen, and one of them has a verse reference to cricket, *Her [he] was the prettiest fellow, at Football or at Cricket*. The words were adapted slightly, from earlier use in a comedy of D'Urfey's that had played the Theatre Royal, as we shall see later on. Interestingly, a few years ago Sotheby's auctioned an edition of the *Pills* that had been owned by the Halle Orchestra's conductor, the late Sir John Barbirolli. He also was a cricket lover.

The Theatre Royal, Drury Lane, provides a tenuous link with what has often been accepted as the first (*sic*) cricket song. The great actor David Garrick's ALL IN THE WRONG was sung there in June 1761. Although *Ye Poets who mount on the fam'd winged steed* has nothing to do with cricket, there are many metrical similarities with what is known as COTTON'S CRICKET SONG. Confusion still surrounds the exact chronology of *Assist all ye muses, and join to rehearse, An old English sport never praised yet in verse*, which was said to have been written by the Rev. Reynell Cotton, Master of Hyde Abbey School, Winchester, for the famous Hambledon Club in 1776. Or was it 1767? It was, if you believe George Huddesford, who reprinted the song in his *Wiccamical Chaplet* in 1804, though Huddesford's was not the first reprint by any means.

The song had appeared in *The Canterbury Journal* for October, 1773; then there was a publication by order of the Hambledon Cricket Club, 5 June, 1781; the Club's minute book reveals a further order for July, 1790 'that Mr Cotton's Cricket Song be Framed and glazed and hung up in the Cricket Club Room, and one hundred copys be printed'; and then the first scorer to the M.C.C., Samuel Britcher, had twice reproduced it in his annual books of scores — 1800 and 1801.

If that is not muddling enough, it should be said that it is doubtful whether Reynell Cotton wrote the song in the first place. In August of 1772, *The Kentish Gazette* had published THE NOBLE GAME OF CRICKET written in consequence of a match between Hampshire and Kent at Bishopsbourne Park, near Canterbury, which Kent won by two wickets. The song which begins *Attend all ye Muses* is virtually identical to Cotton's version, except that there are Kentish names 'praised yet in verse' instead of those from Hampshire.

It would seem that Cotton's is the parody, though it is possible that both versions are topical adaptations of an earlier evergreen. 'The old English Sport', of course, had been praised before in verse, and the song, at least Cotton's version of it, has since many times found its way into books on cricket, occasionally with the traditional tune that accompanies 'King John and the Abbot'.

Cotton was a one-time President of the Hambledon Club, and several of the team had musical inclinations, notably John Small, regarded as 'one of the greatest batsmen of his age'. Small changed his profession from shoemaker to that of making bats and balls, as the board on his doorway testified:

> *Here lives John Small,*
> *Makes bats and balls,*
> *Pitches a wicket, plays at cricket*
> *With any man in England.*

He also excelled at skating, shooting and walking! Apparently he used to take regular seven-mile treks until his mid-eighties — he was for many years a gamekeeper on the Greatham and Foley Manor. Small's musical proclivities consisted of playing bass viol in the Petersfield Choir for seventy-five years, and also tenor violin 'without the aid of spectacles' in the last twelve months of his life. His sons, John and Eli, both cricketers and 'capital musicians', were also incumbents of the Petersfield Choir.

Small Snr. once received a beautifully-made violin from the Duke of Dorset, and sent in return some equally beautifully made bats and balls. The story goes that on crossing two or three fields on his way to a musical engagement, Small encountered a savage bull who charged at him, whereupon 'our hero with the characteristic coolness and presence of mind of a good cricketer, began playing upon his bass, to the admiration and perfect satisfaction of the mischievous beast'.

Other versions have him playing a violin instead of a bass viol, and without a handy tree stump upon which to squat it does seem to be stretching the Stradivarius, but why spoil a good story!

The Hambledon Club's chronicler, John Nyren, was himself a musician who attended soirées at the house of Vincent Novello (of the music publishing family) where were to be found *literateurs* and composers of the day — Hazlitt, Shelley, Dickens, Lamb, Leigh Hunt, Cowden Clarke, Mendelssohn and J. B. Cramer. Nyren's early musical gatherings had been equally selective. As a youngster he had played fiddle to local gipsies to earn 'protection' for his father's chickens. In *The Cricketers of My Time* he rhapsodises over the tenor voice of wicket-keeper Tom Sueter 'which for sweetness, power, and purity of tone would, with proper cultivation have made him a handsome fortune. With what rapture have I hung upon his notes when he has given us a hunting song in the Club-room after the day's practice was over'. Sueter used to join in many a glee with long-stop 'Little' George Leer of 'the sweet counter-tenor voice' at the 'Bat and Ball' on Broadhalfpenny. Harmony cemented, no doubt, by perils shared in stopping vicious 'curlers and twisters'.

The après-cricket activities at Hambledon echoed the traditional complement to a day's exertion in the field. A most necessary slaking of thirst was accompanied sometimes by an organised singing contest as is to be seen in the *Hampshire Chronicle* of 20 May, 1782, which advertises a match combining the forces of Alresford and Odiham against Hampshire on Odiham Down:

'Likewise will be given gratis, by T. Webb of the George, Odiham, A Silver Punch Ladle, to be sung for by Companies who are Players in the above match, on the evening of the first day of the match at half-past seven o'clock.

The company that best performs three songs and a catch in two or more parts to have the prize.

Also a Silver Table Spoon to the Person that performs three solo songs the best.

Each company to have an umpire with them, by whom the prizes will be decided.

Copies of what they intend to sing to be delivered to T. Webb, by ten o'clock in the forenoon of the day of singing.'

Both Sueter and Leer appeared for Hampshire in this match, and they must each have been well-backed in the solo singing contest. Could the early delivery of copies be for the landlord to practise an accompaniment, or did he want to act as censor to the more vulgar lyrics?

An example of the bibulous nature of cricket songs is underlined in Harman's collection on *Bucks Dialect*. THE RADNAGE CRICKET SONG from the Chilterns was one of the earliest of the survivors, and its continued existence is helped by a recent arrangement with piano accompaniment by Madeleine Campbell:

> *And now the game is ended, boys,*
> *And we have won the ball,*
> *The very next time we come this way*
> *We'll give this house a call.*

Chatteris, in the Fen country, is known more for its boxers, Eric Boon and Dave 'Boy' Green, than for its cricketers, yet in the summer of 1791 the reverse was true. Not that they were very successful, as both their games against the Manea Club in the Isle of Ely were lost, as this song reveals:

CRICKET SONG
Tune — "White Cockade"
(trad. Scottish)

1 *In seventeen hundred and ninety-one*
'Twas on the twenty-first of June,
The Chatteris lads to Manea came,
All for to play the cricket game.
With their bats held up, like bold young men,
As they came marching into town,
Whilst their fiddles playing, and thus they said —
Come now, my boys, for the blue cockade.

2 *About three o'clock in the afternoon*
They all did meet upon the green,
And the Manea lads so boldly played
That they fairly won the blue cockade.
So neatly they did bat and catch,
By winning this great cricket match;
Seven men they had for to go in,
And thus the blue cockade did win.

3 *It was only the twenty-ninth of June,*
To Chatteris went the Manea men,
With them to play the other game,
And there likewise came off with fame.
Altho' four fresh men Chatteris choosed,
The Manea lads did not refuse,
But with courage true the game they played,
Saying, Now, my boys for the blue cockade.

4 *The match of eleven each side did play,*
And the Manea lads they won the day;
At Chatteris, when the game was through,
They beat them notches thirty-two.
Then up into the town they went,
All for a little merryment;
And at night came home with balls and bats,
With blue cockades upon their hats.

Ent⁴. Stat⁵. Hall. — Price 2/6

London, Printed & Sold at Bland & Wellers Music Warehouse, 23, Oxford St.

This lively piece no doubt decorated the piano lids of many moderately talented performers. The front cover, depicting a charming rural scene with musician and dancers in front of a tent, children playing cricket with two stump wickets in front of a pub, a school and church in the background, and a goat in the foreground, is thought to be the first visual link between cricket and music.

The Rondo was published between 1812 and 1815, and is by Matthias Holst, who later inserted 'von' before his surname, borrowed illegally from one of his cousins who had been knighted for diplomacy. Matthias Holst, part German, part Swedish, was born in 1769, lived first in Riga, and then early in the nineteenth century emigrated to England. He was married to a Russian, Katharina Rogge, and was an industrious though not very original composer. He died in 1854, and is buried in Highgate Cemetery. He was the great grandfather of Gustav Holst, composer of 'The Planets'.

Royman Browne found the inspiration for this drawing from an article by John Arlott:

1 *They tell of Brown of Brighton*
  Before the days of Grace
  Whose bowling used to frighten
  The batsman by its pace.

2 *His underarm was faster*
  Or so they used to say
  Than any man could master
  Who met him in his day

3   One ball made him history
    A legend of the past
    Fact and half a mystery
    The fastest of the fast

4   Past the bat rising steeper
    It rose above the bails
    On past the wicket keeper
    According to the tales

5   Long stop had no chance at all
    He only heard it pass
    Heard it go, that howling ball
    That never touched the grass

6   One man, brave to do it
    Spread out his greatcoat wide
    The ball just burst on through it,
    Killed a dog on t'other side.

This is the first half of a song which was first heard in 1977 on a BBC Radio 3 programme 'The Sound of Bat and Ball'. The lyrics are by John Arlott and they were set to music by The Yetties, those engaging entertainers from Yetminster, Dorset.

The incident so described happened in a match at Lords *circa* 1818. Apparently George Brown's underarm bowling was so fast that most of the fielders were placed behind the wicket in order to try and field the unintentional deflections from the bat. When Brown played for Brighton, the long stop 'Little' Dench used to attach a sack of straw to his chest as protection. He once took five wickets in five successive balls, and at another occasion on Walderton Common threw a cricket ball 137 yards. He was 6 ft 2½ inches tall, between fifteen and eighteen stone, and the father of seventeen children.

SEE THE CRICKETERS OF KENT

1   'See the cricketers of Kent
    all in white
    with delight
    play before the shady tent.

2   Mind the bowler in the vale
    Pitched with strength
    there's a length
    mark the shivering of the bale.

3   Now the batsman stands complete
    sends the ball
    over all,
    scores six notches for the feat'

The first three of a seven verse part song, with a musical setting for two tenors and bass by Samuel Porter, *circa* 1825. The words were written by J. Burnby in the eighteenth century.

A CRICKET SONG ON THE MATCH WHEN THE NOTTINGHAM PLAYED THE SHEFFIELD AND LEICESTER CLUBS AT DARNALL, JULY 1826 IN WHICH MARSDEN SCORED FROM HIS OWN BAT 227 RUNS AT ONE INNINGS

'What's the matter, my friends, at Sheffield to-day,
That most of the people are going away?
What's the matter, indeed! — why, don't you know, Mester,
That Nottingham's playing both Sheffield and Leicester.
    Hey derry, derry down, etc.

'So as I had heard it reported by many,
That Cricket was finest diversion of any,
I thought, just for once, I'd join in their fun;
And to Darnall I got, as the stirrings begun.

'When Rawlins and Marsden began to get warm,
The Nottingham Batters were filled with alarm;
For down went their stumps, *with a terrible crash,*
And soon was extinguished the Nottingham flash.

'Then old Father Dennis, enraged, took his Bat,
In wonder whatever his comrades were at;
But Tom tipt *his stumps, in double quick time,*
And made the old boy with a round 0 to shine.

'Thus man followed man, in rapid succession,
And the score *but slowly was making progression;*
The knowing ones *strangely were alter'd in looks,*
And seemed very anxious to alter their books.

'Davis, Barber, and Vincent, with one or two more,
Soon made for the Union a very good score.
Then Marsden went in, in his glory and pride,
And the arts of the Nottingham Players defied.

'Oh, Marsden, at Cricket, is nature's perfection,
For hitting the Ball in any direction;
He ne'er fears his Wicket, so safely he strikes,
And he does with the Bat and the Ball what he likes.

'Next, Gamble came forward, aspiring for fame,
And for ever establish'd at Cricket his name;
He kept up his Wicket, that day and the next,
And Barker and Clarke were bothered and vext.

'For Tom kept hitting the ball in the crowd,
Who in its applause grew boisterous and loud;
Then in praises of Gamble grew equally mad —
Oh! thou'rt nought but a good one, little Gamble, my lad!

'But I said 'twere a shame, and I don't understand
Why you don't give a shout for yon Kettleband,
For wherever a Ball is struck out on the green
There's sure to be him and his striped breeches seen.

'So for Kettleband, quickly we give a good shout,
But Tom, turning round, said, let him look out;
Then he drove the Ball right over the people,
Some thought 'twere going o'er Handsworth Church steeple.

'Then homewards I trudged to our country folks,
To tell 'em a few of the Cricketers' jokes;
But that joke of Tom Marsden's will ne'er be forgot,
When Two Hundred and Twenty-Seven Notches he got.

'For Marsden and Gamble we fill up our glasses,
As brimful as when we toast favourite lasses,
And then drank success to all Cricketers true,
Who with honour this noble diversion pursue.'

The verses sung by a local poet were published as a broadside. The Darnall Ground, three miles from the centre of Sheffield, apparently accommodated 25,000 people during the match who saw the combined forces of Sheffield and Leicester win by an innings and 203 runs, even though five of the team failed to score.

Tom Marsden, a Sheffield brickmaker, was a devastating left-handed hitter. A reporter for the *Doncaster, Notts, and Lincoln Gazette* later wrote: 'When handling the bat it appears nothing more than a common walking-stick to him'.

'The principal object of the volume now respectfully submitted to the public, is to obviate the complaint frequently made, at the festive board, of a dearth of sporting songs.' So Charles Armiger from Great Melton in Norfolk, editor of *Howitt's British Preserve*, did introduce to British Sportsmen 'a class alike distinguished for liberality and intelligence' his *Vocal Cabinet* in July, 1830. Yet out of 'an extensive collection of scarce, curious, and original songs and ballads there is but one on cricket. Anonymously from the eighteenth century came THE CRICKETER:

> *To live a life, free from gout, pain, or phthisic,*
> *Athletic employment is found the best physic;*
> *The nerves are by exercise hardened and strengthened*
> *And vigour attends it, by which life is lengthened.*
> *Derry down, etc.*

The CRICKETER'S SONG written by Daniel H. C. Nelson and sung at one of the meetings of the East Surry (*sic*) Cricket Club in the season of 1831, is inventive, humorous, and very long. It is similar to many that give a verse apiece to members of the Club, most of whose names are unknown outside their immediate circle. Nelson's song, however, does have one verse that strikes a resonant chord:

> *For Euphony's sake it were p'rhaps quite as well,*
> *If I did not the name of this Cricketer tell;*
> *But his deeds in the field are so worthy of fame,*
> *That I care not a pin for his jaw-breaking name;*
> *So WANOSTROCHT promptly I'll venture to dub*
> *A model for all, and the Pink of our Club.*

The ubiquitous and versatile Nicholas Wanostrocht, or Felix as he was known, will be found presenting one of his own offerings later in these pages.

The Death
OF THE
Ashby-de-la-Zouch
CRICKET CLUB.
A SONG.
Tune,—" Maggie Lawder."

A.D. 1827.

WHEN last we met, who would have thought
   This Club so soon would end, Sir,
That Discord could so soon have wrought
   Such strife among such friends, Sir ?
Alas ! that I, who sang the Birth
   Last year, (O, what a rub, Sir,)
Should this year have to sing the Death
   Of the ASHBY CRICKET CLUB, Sir.

Perhaps some Critic grave may say,
   " Mistaken is your mirth, Sir,
" More solemn ought your dirge to be,
   " Than when you sang the Birth, Sir."
But if, my friends, it is decreed,
   This Club shall lose its Breath, Sir,
You'll think, I hope, it ought indeed,
   To have a merry Death, Sir.

How Discord crept with giant stride,
   In vain I strove to find, Sir ;
A friend of mine came in and cried
   " By Jove you must be blind, Sir,
" I'll quickly ease you of your doubt,
   " And lead you thro' the mist, Sir,
" Look o'er these names, you'll soon find out
   " Five Lawyers on the list, Sir."

" 'Tis clear," I cried, " and well explain'd,
   " And all my doubts are o'er, Sir ;"
Five Lawyers in a Club, untrain'd,
   Are quite enough, and more, Sir ;
For I have read, I know right well,
   (The story made a rout, Sir,)
How two had nearly upset Hell,
   And kick'd the Devil out, Sir.

While life remains, hope still is high,
   And I would fain believe, Sir,
That tho' this Club is doom'd to die,
   You'll grant it a Reprieve, Sir ;
But if resolv'd the Blow to strike,
   Let's hope, while now it dies, Sir,
That from its ashes, Phœnix like,
   It may with vigour rise, Sir.

FINIS.

Beadsmoores, Printers, Ashby.

The Ashby Club was not the only one to have trouble with 'lawyers'. A song about the match played at F. T. Bircham's, Burhill Park, Esher, thirty years later tells how there they kept the LAWYERS OUT OF MISCHIEF

> *The Lawyers went in and the first case was called on:*
> *An action for battery and grievous assault.*
> *And 'Burnett v Garth' was a cause which ne'er palled on*
> *The mind of a cricketer worthy his salt.*
>
> *How many had verdicts against them for trespass,*
> *Were 'stumped', and 'run out', I can't very well say;*
> *Or what were their colours (for I let their dress pass);*
> *This I know, that a few were caught out by 'ca. sa.'.*

Ireland is not a country that rates high in cricket consciousness, yet in the early 1830s there were a couple of songs that emerged from Kilkenny in the South West. They were written to celebrate two victories by the Kilkenny Club over their rivals from Ballinasloe and one learns with a total lack of surprise, they were sung in an evening of 'Tipsy mirth and revelry':

> *And now, my boys, give one cheer more.*
> *For Bat, Ball, Bails, and Wicket,*
> *While I propose the three great C's,*
> **KILKENNY, CLARET, CRICKET.**

There is also a song from the North called DUNGIVEN CRICKET MATCH, which sets the scene of an encounter between the local side and Derry.

Two songs honouring players of the time, almost certainly written by John Baxter, who was the first to use an inking roller for printing. His son George (b. 1804), invented an oil colour printing process, and was an engraver of coloured prints. They could have joined forces in the production of these songs. MY FRIENDS LEAVE YOUR WORK NOW TO SPORT AND TO PLAY is probably the earlier, and SING MUSE THE MAN,

circa 1839-40. 'Honest' Baxter of Surrey, in the song, is no relation.

John Baxter lived in Lewes where he was a printer and publisher, and in 1809 produced a pamphlet on the Laws of Cricket. It is thought likely that he was the 'ghost' writer for two of the earliest books of instruction on the game by Boxall and Lambert, viz. 'There's the knowing Will Lambert a man of great fame'.

Benjamin Aistabie was Honorary Secretary to the Marylebone Club from 1822 until his death in 1842. An old Etonian, who featured in the pages of *Tom Brown's School days*, he was a wine merchant by trade, and was of huge bulk. His twenty stone made him a comic figure on the cricket field, nevertheless a redoubtable good humour outweighed all physical disadvantages, and his ready wit was put to good use in several songs and rhymes that he composed on the characters of the day.

The same kind of wittiness was the common feature of many of the songs that now arrived. In many cases their success was limited and of short duration, because to understand the innuendos and implications of the lyrics necessitated fairly intimate knowledge of the characters in the song. Be that as it may, it was from around this period, the 1830s and 40s, that there was a steadily increasing trickle of songs on the game. A number gave the words only, with perhaps the name of the tune; they appeared in sporting papers and magazines, club annuals, and as a complement to books of scores and instruction. THE CRICKETERS CLUB (for Lords and Commons), THE OLD ENGLISH CRICKETER (Bell's Life), and SLOWMAN'S CHANT (Teignbridge C.C.) are just three of these. As the century wore on, and as facilities for printing, and book and music reproduction improved, and as the parlour and drawing-room with its Victorian aspidistra became the centre of family entertainment and the respectable 'thing to do', so did the marketing of songs with accompaniment for the pianoforte become a profitable exercise. No matter that the pianoforte was more often a Broadwood than a Bechstein — likely as not the rendition could not be helped.

But before the beery baritones are really set loose with specially arranged accompaniments, we ought to note a few more important contributions to cricket song. One came from Samuel Reynolds Hole, M.A., D.D., Dean of Rochester, who for a time was Chaplain to the Archbishop of Canterbury. He was the Donald Soper of his day, a popular preacher and platform orator. He also liked to hunt, write about rose-growing, and place bets on the results of cricket matches. There is a line in one of Aistabies' songs '*Hole put the great pot on*', which caused great hilarity for those who knew Hole. Having taken a bet, he used to pace up and down in a state of considerable excitement and anxiety, even though the amount ventured was very small.

Hole composed his Cricket song while at Oxford in 1842, and sang it to the satisfaction of his undergraduate friends 'vociferously expressed'.

Over fifty years later when replying to an invitation to sing the song again, he wrote: 'I no longer perform in public, but if we are to have the music on the 8th of April, and some kind vocalist would chirp my verses, clearly as the Cricket upon the hearth, I venture to hope that the company would join the Chorus.' The last verse to the Air 'YE MARINERS OF ENGLAND goes:

Long, long, on lawn of noble,
And in the cottage field,
This game of games to English hearts
Its healthful joys shall yield;
And oft at eve, when stumps are drawn,
The fragrant weed shall glow;
As ye tell, how they fell,
Where the ripping swift uns go;
Or the crafty Clarke with peerless twist
Sends in his teazers slow.

The crafty Clarke, of course, was none other than William Clarke of Nottingham, the autocratic founder of the famous touring All-England XI. His baffling under-arm bowling which bewildered the best bats in the land, enabled him to take an average of 340 wickets each year from 1847 to 1853. Nicholas Wanostrocht — 'Felix' — thought he had found the answer, so he produced a booklet called *How to Play Clarke*. There are only two or three known copies, so perhaps Clarke bought the remainder of the stock and had it burned!

Around this period there was involvement with the game from another with virtually the same surname. William Mark Clark, wholesale bookseller and publisher of Warwick Lane, and Red Lion Court off Fleet Street in London, produced sporting handbooks on pedestrianism and wrestling, boxing, and cricket which, so we are led to believe, ran to fifteen editions. He published also volumes of songs under titles such as *Giant Warbler; Orphean Warbler*, and *Sporting Songs*, 'containing 100 of the most approved Sporting Songs extant'. The only way there could possibly be any confusion between the two Clark(e)s lies in a book by William Bolland that was published in 1851, entitled *Cricket Notes; with a letter containing practical hints, by William Clark.* The William C. in this case was most certainly the master bowler from Nottingham — a publishing oversight caused the omission of the letter 'e'.

Clarke, who had lost the use of an eye early in his life, was an extremely caustic customer. A lady once told him that she thought her son would make an excellent cricketer as he 'stood six feet in his stockings'. 'Dear me, what a large number of toes he must have' was the sardonic riposte.

He used to sing a cricket song to the tune of 'Rule Britannia'. The second verse went:

> *The Marylebone ranks first of all,*
> *It's they who do our laws enrol;*
> *And then I Zingari, those trumps with bat and ball,*
> *And the Eleven of All-England, composed of great and small*

(Refrain)
> *Then success to cricket, 'tis a noble game,*
> *It's patronised by royalty, and men of wealth and fame.*

It may seem false modesty for Clarke to put his own All-England Eleven behind one of the oldest of the wandering clubs, I Zingari, however the Gypsies were a force with which to be reckoned. Formed in 1845, membership is carefully selective, one of the rules being 'That the Entrance be nothing, and that the Annual Subscription do not exceed the Entrance.' W. P. Bolland, of the previously mentioned *Cricket Notes* was appointed Perpetual President by the founders J. Loraine Baldwin, R.P. Long, the Hon, F. Ponsonby, later Lord Bessborough, and Sir Spencer Ponsonby-Fane. Ponsonby-Fane was for many years treasurer to the M.C.C., and his association with Lords spanned eighty years. He had played cricket with William Ward, M.P. to the City of London, who had purchased the lease of Lords in 1825. He started the unique pictorial collection which continues to fascinate visitors to the ground today, and he had taken part in the first Canterbury Cricket Week. Later in his life, Ponsonby-Fane also had written the words to THE CRICKETERS CAROL with music by H. Preston-Thomas. Several members of the newly-formed I Zingari Club had performed in the theatricals and games at the Canterbury Cricket Week since its inception, and a link was forged that still remains. It was at a C.C. Week that the I.Z. Song, written by P.P.,

The 84th Regiment amalgamated with the 65th in 1881, to become The York and Lancaster Regiment.

W. Bolland was performed. The fact that a rule of the Club allowed field directions to be conveyed in French or Italian was not an excuse for foreign tongues to infiltrate such a God-given chance for jingoism:

> *We are told England's armies assembled,*
> *When Liberty's cause was in view,*
> *We are told too that tyranny trembled*
> *'Neath the folds of the Red, White and Blue;*
> *Yes! the Red, White and Blue o'er the Ocean*
> *Has floated in conquests of old,*
> *But tonight let us pledge our devotion*
> *To the folds of the Red, Black and Gold*

A fundamental accoutrement to the theatrical entertainments and country house Balls was the music provided by military bands and dance ensembles. Regimental bands from the 39th and 74th, Mount's Celebrated Quadrille Band, even a band under the direction of the temperamental and eccentric Louis Jullien, who did so much to popularise the Promenade Concert in this country. He too, by the way, wrote a CRICKET POLKA, only it portrayed the insect not the game.

The continued connection between the I Zingari Club and the Canterbury Cricket Week gave plenty of opportunity for bandmasters and song writers to plug their latest galop, march, waltz and ditty simply by dedicating the composition to the Club, or incorporating the word 'Zingari' into the title. The publishers also realised their chance to capitalise by housing the music in beautifully reproduced coloured front covers.

This scene is of a Test Match between England and Australia at Lords, though the composition of fifty-two characters is imaginary. The painting was by G. H. Barrable and R. Ponsonby Staples in 1887. Amongst the participants on the field are T. W. Garrett of Australia fielding the ball, W. G. Grace and W. W. Read, the batsmen, Blackham keeping wicket, and F. R. Spofforth, the bowler. The onlookers make a distinguished gathering. Included with their Royal Highnesses, the Prince and Princess of Wales, are the Duchess of Leinster, the Earl of Bessborough, Lord Harris, nine Knights, two Honourables, two Generals, a Captain, a Doctor of Philosophy, an M.P., two Ladies, and Mrs. Langtry.

Lady Emily Peel, who died in 1924, was married to Sir Robert Peel, the eldest son of *the* Robert Peel, who founded the London Police Force.

CRICKET.

Words by
HARRY & LEO TREVOR.

Music by
A. SCOTT-GATTY.

1. Old Eng-land's great boast I pro-pose as a toast: "Here's to crick-et of ev-er-y kind, From the
2. If you've the bad luck to get stumped for a duck, Or dis-missed by a gal-ler-y catch, Pray

Copyright 1898 by Boosey & Co.

H. 2217

swell coun-ty bat to the small rus-tic flat, And bet-ter men no-where you'll
don't moon a-bout, or de-clare you were out To the ve-ry worst ball in the

find............ 'Tis nice, to be sure, to pile up a big score, Or to
match............ Don't swear at the ball, in fact, don't swear at all, Do not

make a long stand at the wick...et, But de-
rave at the state of the wick...et, You

.feat is no shame if you play the right game, So
are not to blame if you play the right game, So

4

CHORUS.

when you play cricket— Play cricket! Then steady's the word! steady's the word!
when you play cricket— Play cricket!

Play cricket! Then steady's the word! steady's the word!

Play cricket! Then steady's the word! steady's the word!

Play cricket! Then steady's the word! steady's the word!

Don't be too anxious to score;...... When the bowl...ing gets loose you can

Don't be too anxious to score;...... When the bowl...ing gets loose you can

Don't be too anxious to score;...... When the bowl...ing gets loose you can

Don't be too anxious to score;...... When the bowl...ing gets loose you can slog like the deuce! So don't be too anx-ious,............

slog like the deuce! Don't be too anx-ious,

slog like the deuce!

slog like the deuce!

Don't be too anx-ious,............ Don't be too anxious to score.

Don't be too anx-ious,............ Don't be too anxious to score.

Don't be too anxious, Don't be too anxious to score.

Don't be too anxious, Don't be too anxious to score.

Cricket.

Another of the bandleaders at Canterbury was Herr Felix who often conducted an Amateur band during the breaks in play, as well as playing violin in the small orchestra that accompanied the entertainment at the Theatre in the evening. Calling bandmasters 'Herr' was a way of ridiculing Prussian militarism that seemed to be imbued in any baton that kept precise Teutonic $\frac{4}{4}$. After all, Felix did have a foreign surname as well — Wanostrocht, of Flemish origin. Wanostrocht had adopted the pseudonym Felix partly to disguise his cricketing activities from the parents of pupils at his Camberwell School, where he had inherited the headmastership, and partly because of the difficulty experienced by all and sundry in pronouncing his surname.

Nicholas Felix seemed good at everything. He had great talent as a writer, draughtsman, artist, musician, actor, inventor, and not least, left-handed all rounder, and all of these activities have been covered in Gerald Brodribb's excellent memoir of 1962, together with the text of the second edition of Felix's own book, *Felix on the Bat*.

Felix combined his literary and musical knowledge in a song composed to celebrate the victory of an English Eleven over a French team in a match played at Dieppe in August, 1864. He used the now time-honoured practice of making adept word-play with the characteristics of each member of the team during the eighteen verses. The chorus is consistently less inventive, and concentrates on *the bowls of Punch that flow*. There is also a quaint and charming homily which Felix penned to his manuscript now residing at Lords. Is there a suggestion between the

SUCCESS TO THE FRIENDS of the BAT AND THE BALL

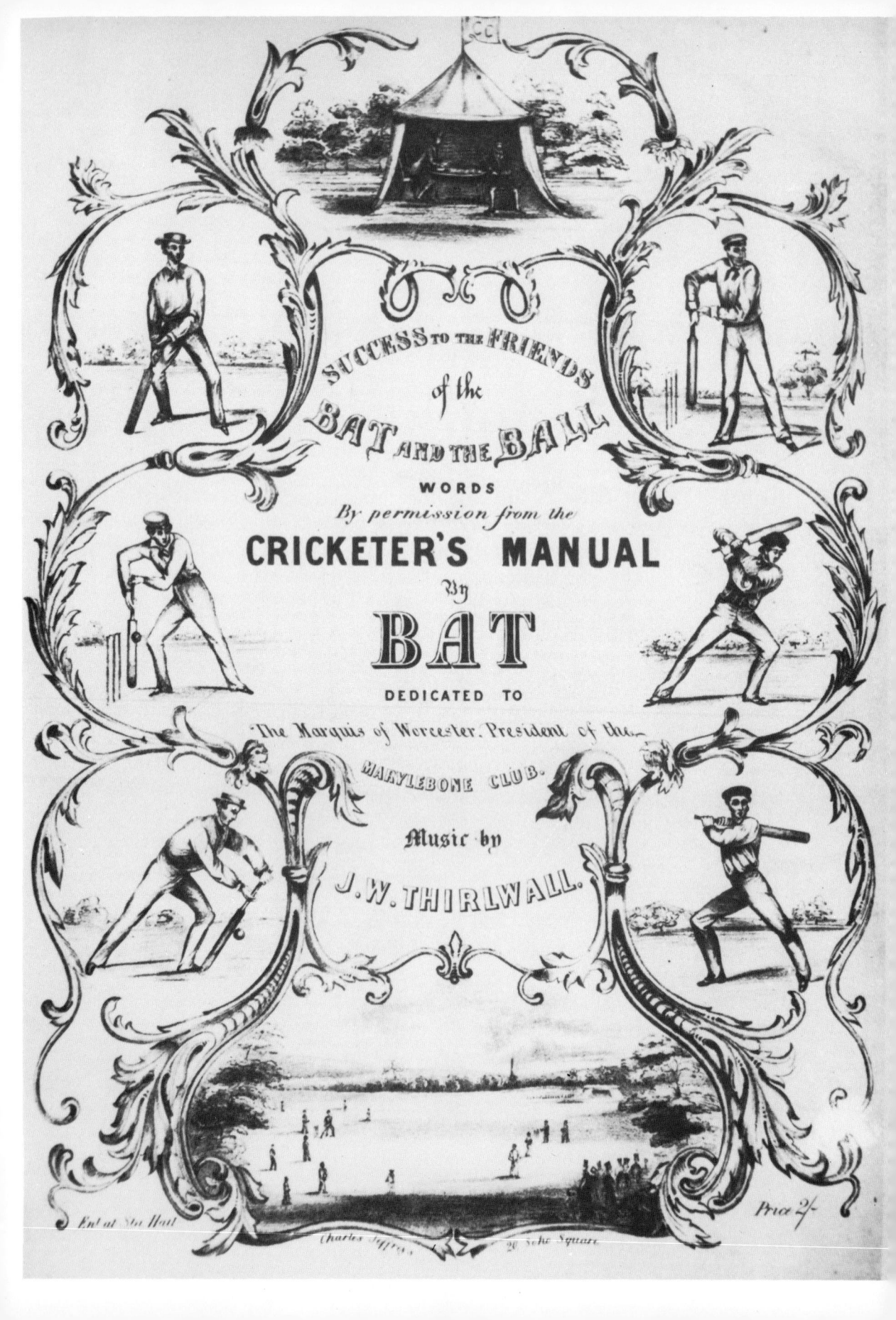

WORDS

By permission from the

CRICKETER'S MANUAL

By

BAT

DEDICATED TO

The Marquis of Worcester, President of the

MARYLEBONE CLUB.

Music by

J. W. THIRLWALL.

lines that some of the team had had too much Punch? '*The Captain here again reminds his hearers of the bad taste of self-praise; commends them to bestow a parting Complement to those of the opposite party who met them in the Field: wishing them the enjoyment of good health: prays that a good and peaceful understanding may long exist to enable France and England to join battle together in defence of their united interests:— and Concluding as is most proper, by proposing three cheers for Her most Gracious Majesty Queen Victoria. By the Grace of God.*

> *Here's a sport that encrimsons with roses the cheek,*
> *Strews a garland of flowers o'er life's chequered day,*
> *Tunes the pulse to sweet music — gives strength to the weak;*
> *Why surely, then cricket is worthy a lay*
> *So fill up a bumper, and joyously call*
> *For success to the friends of the bat and the ball!*

The SONG OF THE CRICKETER was one of a number of songs that found their way into the writings of Charles Box, sometime editor of cricket for *The Times*. Box, enjoyed the anonymity of 'Bat' when he produced his *Cricketer's Manual* from 1848 to 51, and the words of this song, written in 1850, appeared in the Manual for the following year. He also included it in his splendid tome on *The English Game of Cricket* which was published in 1877. There we learn that besides a musical setting by J. W. Thirlwall, there was another by one Herr Meyer Lutz. Box prefaced the song with the information that the Duke of Wellington once remarked to the House of Lords that his success in arms was owing, in a great measure, to the manly sports of Great Britain, and one sport above all — cricket.

In *The English Game of Cricket* there is an EVENING SONG also written in 1850 and set to music by Box himself, and there as well THE 'VEXED BOWLER' which is the identical title of one of two cricketing songs that have survived from J. D. Mills, who was a printer and a publisher in Wandsworth. Mills, who had produced a pocket edition of the Laws of Cricket in 1848, used the tune of *The Gay Cavalier* for his song about a bowler who lost his 'rag' as the batsman foiled his every trick:

> *'I see plain', he then swore,*
> *As it was hit for four*

Inevitably, the moral arrives:

Just learn to keep cool,
And your temper rule,
Or you may be knock'd about for a week.

Mills' other song THE 'TIE MATCH', borrowed an instantly forgettable tune that was all the rage in the eighteen fifties, 'Trab, Trab', and indeed CRICKETING'S ALL THE RAGE was the title used for a new song that had emanated from the North-East:

Durham City has been dull so long,
No bustle at all to show;
But now the rage of all the throng
Is at cricketing to go.
Long-Field, Long-Stop, Bowl or Bat,
All different posts engage;
Ball struck — not caught — a notch for that,
O Cricketing's all the rage.

The tale is of 'youths at play' on Durham Sands Racecourse (where Robert Percival once threw a cricket ball over 140 yards, and found a niche in Wisden) where they are watched by 'blooming nymphs' standing by, their 'lover's heat to engage' for games of another sort in Keepier Wood.

There were quite a few songs on cricket now coming from the North. Two from Lascelles Hall, a small village near Huddersfield, which in the days before the county championship became fully operational, had a side that could beat the best in the surrounding districts. Both songs recount famous victories. HERE'S TO LASCELLES HALL by E. A. Lodge told of the time they won the Heavy Woollen District Cup having beaten Hartshead, Staincliffe, Batley, and Ossett, and OH THE SHEFFIELDERS by a local poet, was a song of triumph after the conquest of Sheffield in September, 1870. Two from Scotland, FLOORS CASTLE CRICKETERS' SONG by W. Swain, P.C., to the tune of Dolly Dobbs which, perhaps unexpectedly, starts with the lines *Of all the games in Scotland, good cricket is the best* (surely little short of sacrilege at a spot where James II of Scotland was blown up by a cannon in 1460), and THE CRICKETERS' GALOP with vocal chorus, by Charles Denney, Bandmaster of the 1st Greenock Renfrewshire Rifle Volunteers, with a dedication to the Greenock West End Cricket Club.

THE CRICKETER'S GALOP

WITH VOCAL CHORUS

THEN HURRAH HURRAH TO OUR GLORIOUS GAME

THEN HURRAH FOR THE BAT BALL AND WICKET

FOR BRITAINS SONS CAN TAKE THE BOAST

IN THE NOBLE GAME OF CRICKET

DEDICATED TO THE

Greenock West End Cricket Club

BY

CHARLES DENNEY

B.M. 1ST GREENOCK RENFREWSHIRE R.V.

GREENOCK
JAMES INGLIS & SONS

Another CRICKET SONG from the North, Lancashire this time, was by Richard Gorton Barlow, leading professional of the Lancashire XI of the 1870s and '80s. Barlow, given immortality with Francis Thompson's famous stanza 'O my Hornby and my Barlow long ago!', also thought a lot of his opening partner:

> *Captain Hornby is the finest man for many miles around*
> *And all his men have brawny arms — their equals can't be found*
> *When cricket time again comes round, we all shall then be seen,*
> *We like the open sunlight best, out in the fields so green.*
>
> (chorus):
> *Out in the green fields, so happy and so gay.*
> *Of all the games we e're did love, cricket's the game for us —*
> *With bats and balls, stumps and bails, we form the wicket glorious.*
> *As books supply the mind with food, the all-inspiring wicket*
> *The body keeps in glowing health. Then three hurrahs for Cricket!*

Albert Neilson Hornby was the dedicatee of one of the two songs on the game that were written and composed by J. Harcourt Smith. The other has become one of the better-known cricket songs, solely on the basis of a recently produced print of the front cover which shows the formidable figure of W. G. Grace preparing to take strike. It is called CRICKET – THE SONG OF THE 'CENTURIES', and was originally produced in 1895 in honour of Grace's one hundredth hundred:

> (chorus):
> *At home or abroad where'er*
> *The Union Jack is known*
> *We've met each friendly rival team*
> *Yet always held our own.*
> *We'll welcome still all comers when*
> *A match can e'ere be made,*
> *For of batters, bowlers, fielders now*
> *With GRACE we're not afraid.*

At the height of his fame Grace seemed to be inundated with dedications from all manner of songwriters hoping to popularise their product. Harcourt Smith's song was dedicated by permission; one wonders

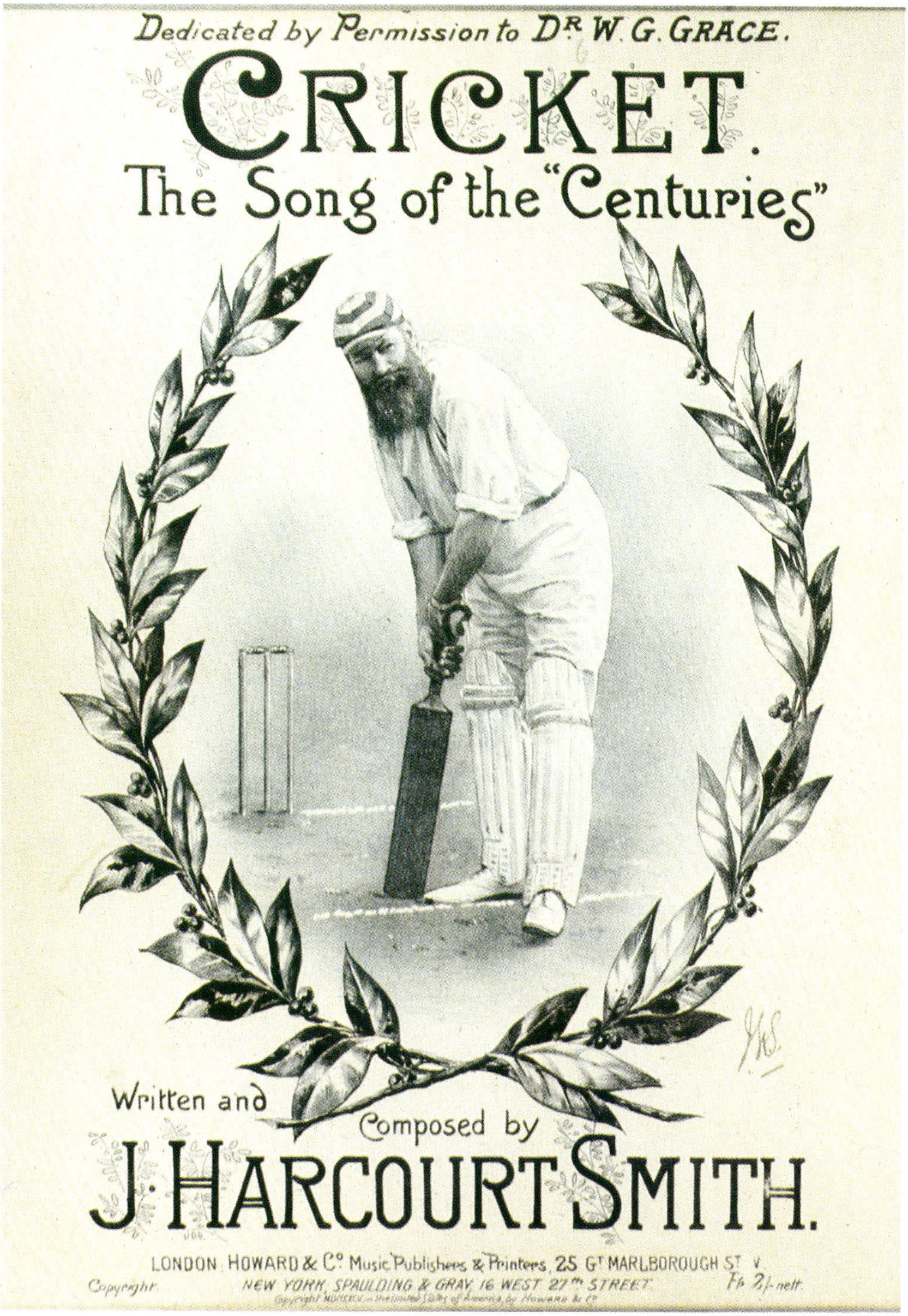
Dedicated by Permission to Dr. W. G. GRACE.
CRICKET.
The Song of the "Centuries"
Written and
Composed by
J. HARCOURT SMITH.
LONDON HOWARD & Co. Music Publishers & Printers, 25 Gt. MARLBOROUGH St. W.
Copyright
NEW YORK, SPAULDING & GRAY 16 WEST 27th STREET
2/- nett

whether some of the others were. If ever a Music Hall song did not need the use of the Great Man's name it is CRICKET AFTER GRACE OR OUT! OUT! OUT!, but there it is, dragged screaming down centre, the topical ploy with the predictability of knock-about comedy:

> *I read the* Daily Telegraph's *account of Doctor Grace,*
> *And thought upon the scroll of fame my name I'd like to place —*
> *I gave a man a five pound note to teach me in a day —*
> *I said my Grace, I took my place, and then prepar'd to play.*(spoken):
> 'Fancy luring me on to cricket! — Why, I'd sooner have had a nice little game of coddam or push-ha'penny. 'Pon my word, I've got cricket on the brain, cricket on the hearth, cricket in the backyard. Why, when I went to bed the other night I couldn't sleep for thinking of it; but when I did get to sleep, I dreamt I was making one big final hit — one slogging hit — then suddenly woke up, and found I was slogging my old woman in the jaw. Oh! I was excited —'

Grace was a National institution and he even became part of THE CRICKETER'S NATIONAL SONG, a choral march with music and words by Frank Thomson. The song was commissioned by J. Curwen and Sons, who were one of a number of music publishers who encapsulated the patriotic fervour that was inherent to late Victorian, early Edwardian England, with a whole succession of songs with redolent phrases such as 'Tis dear old England's National Game', 'For in the

"THE CRICKET BAT POLKA"

By HENRY A. SUTCH

DEDICATED BY PERMISSION TO

DR W. G. GRACE
(THE CHAMPION)

London, CHARLES SHEARD & Co. Music Publishers & Printers, 192, High Holborn, W.C.

Copyright

Price, 3/-
Duet 4/-
Full Orchestra 2/-
Septett 1/-
Odd Parts 2d Each
Full Brass Band, 2/6
Full Military Band 3/-

This Song may be Sung in Public without fee or Licence, Except at Music Halls.

"CRICKET AFTER GRACE,"
OR, OUT! OUT! OUT!

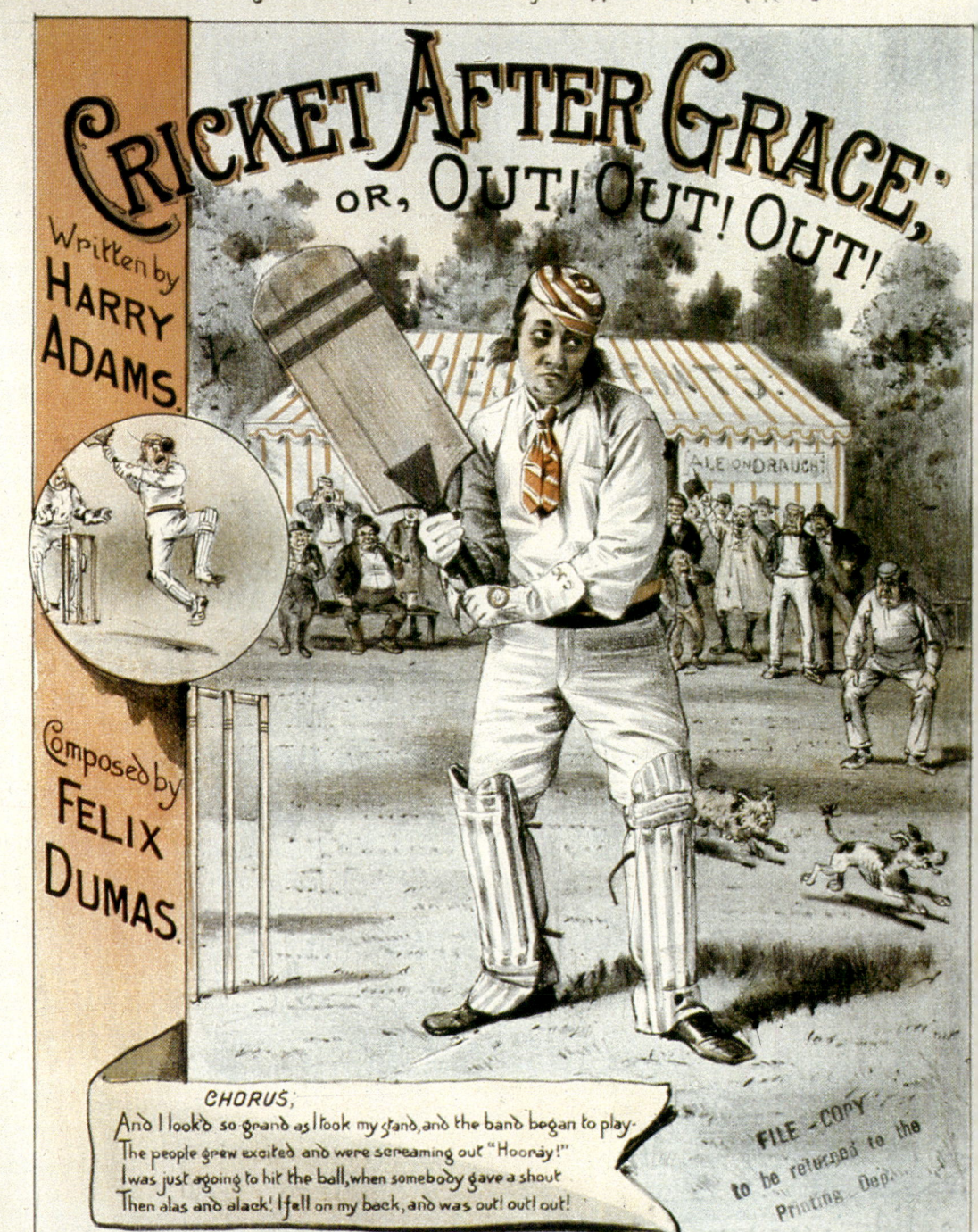

Written by HARRY ADAMS.

Composed by FELIX DUMAS.

CHORUS.
And I look'd so grand as I took my stand, and the band began to play,
The people grew excited and were screaming out "Hooray!"
I was just agoing to hit the ball, when somebody gave a shout
Then alas and alack! I fell on my back, and was out! out! out!

W. P. DEMPSEY.

LONDON: FRANCIS, DAY & HUNTER, 195, OXFORD ST. W.
Publishers of Smallwood's Celebrated Pianoforte Tutor, Smallwood's 55 Melodious Exercises Etc.

NEW YORK. T. B. HARMS & Co 18, EAST 22ND STREET
Copyright MDCCCXCV in the United States of America by Francis, Day & Hunter.

Copyright — Price 4/-

English cricket field unitedly they stand', and 'If you want to see the British Lion play'. Curwen's, and notably the publishing houses of Chester's and Weekes, realised the appeal of these sentiments, and produced choruses for mixed, equal and unison voices that found a virtually captive market in the many Amateur and School choirs throughout the country.

Another common element in songs of this period, and indeed earlier, was to extol the virtues of cricket as opposed to any other game. So we get verses such as in THE CRICKETERS by Kent Sutton:

> *In Canada they have la crosse,*
> *The Yankee has his baseball*
> *Australia has her 'boating'*
> *And the Scotsmen of course 'football'*
> *The Frenchman likes his 'fencing foils'*
> *The Spaniard his 'bull baiting'*
> *The German his 'gymnastics'*
> *And in Norway they love 'skating'*
> *But to my mind there's none can beat —*

And we all know what none can beat. A certain William Flockton thought the same:

> *You may boast of the pleasures untold,*
> *Of football and boldly uphold,*
> *Your bowls, and your 'goff' and your hockey set off*
> *Or the merits of tennis unfold.*
> *So here's to the bat and here's to the ball*
> *And hurrah for the game above all.*

Cricket even conquered the lure of games indoors:

> *I like a game of billiards upon the cloth so green*
> *I don't object to a game of draughts but at that*
> *I'm not o'er keen*
> *But if you should ask the game I love without a doubt I'd say*
> *It is to play in a cricket match upon a lovely day.*
>
> (CRICKET, H. G. L. Mills)

Charles T. West was one of those composers who had written a cricket chorus for equal voices, but he found greater kudos from two of his compositions attached to the exotic figure of Prince 'Ranji', later Maharajah the Jam Sahib of Nawanager. The adventurous Indian Prince who wielded his bat like a scimitar, and who was a dominant force in English cricket at the turn of the century, was second only to Grace in capturing space on music covers. West wrote both words and music for the song RANJI, issued around 1895 by Lyon and Hall of Brighton and Hove; obviously an enterprising local venture with Ranjitsinhji in his first season as a member of the Sussex County side:

> *I sing a glorious hero bold, his name well known to fame;*
> *A man of might in friendly fight, in our fine old English game;*
> *A Prince of our Indian Empire, the willow he wields with ease,*
> *And with practised skill and right good will, he scores his centuries.*
>
> (chorus):
> *Ran – ji – tsinh – ji,*
> *All the way from Inji.*
> *Right well he plays, and earns our praise,*
> *Ranji, Ranjitsinhji;*
> *'Cuts' for three, and 'smacks' for four,*
> *Soon to the century mounts his score,*
> *And loud the crowd then shout and roar*
> *Bravo! Bravo! Ranji!*
>
> *In Batting he strikes out bold and free, and has earned a noble place,*
> *Among our century-makers he is* Abel *to match with GRACE;*
> *The bowlers all their arts may try, their 'breaks' are all in vain,*
> *In the first innings making his century, IN THE SECOND HE'LL DO IT AGAIN.*
>
> (chorus):
> *Ranjitsinhji, etc.*
>
> *His fielding too is sharp and good, when at his 'point' he stands,*
> *He knows his part, and will quickly dart, and the catch is in his hands;*
> *But still at the wicket we like him best, such WINNING ways has he,*
> *Though foreign his name in this English game he's certainly one of we.*
>
> (chorus):
> *Ranjitsinhji, etc.*

Dedicated by special permission to his Highness Prince RANJITSINHJI.

'Ranji.'

By permission of Messrs. E. Hawkins & Co., Brighton.

New Song,

WORDS AND MUSIC BY

C. T. West.

2/- Nett.

LYON and HALL, BRIGHTON and HOVE.

Entered at Stationers Hall.

This Song may be sung in public except at Theatres and Music Halls.

Hurrah! for our glorious hero bold, with the Hindustani name,
'Centurion' he well named may be, in our fine old English game,
Long may he play, and prosper well, each year good fortune bring,
He plays with pluck, and deserves good luck, and we hope to see him King!
(chorus):

Ran — ji — tsinh — ji,
Somewhere out in Inji,
Cricket they'll play there every day,
Led by Ranjitsinhji;
Not in 'battle'-ing use their might,
But in BATTING they'll take delight,
In peace reign he, for his centuree,
Good King Ranjitsinhji!

Two years later, in 1897, Charles West cashed in on his success with the song, and having obtained permission from Messrs. Lyon and Hall, borrowed the tunes from it to produce RANJITSINHJI WALTZ for the London publishing firm of Weekes and Co.

The pages of the magazine *Cricket* in 1899 include a humorous ditty, which reveal perhaps a hint of anxiety as to whether or not Ranjitsinhji would return to the county. The previous winter he had toured Australia with the England side.

A SUSSEX WELCOME TO THE WANDERER
(Air: Oh Willie, we have missed you)
Oh, Ranji is it you dear
Safe again at Hove
They said it was not true dear
That India was your love
Oh, Ranji we have missed you
Why did you rove
Oh, Ranji we have missed you
Welcome back to Hove.

Two decades after this affectionate re-welcome, Ranjitsinhji was the

RANJITSINHJI
WALTZ

COMPOSED BY

Charles T. West.

Composer of the
POPULAR SONG "RANJI" 4/=

Ent: Sta: Hall.　　　　　*C.T.W.*　　　　　Price 4/-

London:
WEEKES & Co. 14, Hanover Street, Regent Street, W.
Chicago, U.S.A., Clayton F. Summy Co., 220, Wabash Avenue.

Copyright, 1897, by Weekes & Co.

recipient of A SONG OF CRICKET, on which he had graciously bestowed his special permission for a dedication, with music by A. H. Behrend, and words by the ex-captain of Surrey, D. L. A. Jephson, one of the last of the lob bowlers. It marked the end of a colourful career.

The line in the second verse of West's song which likened Ranji to Abel reminds us that he too, one of the outstanding cricketers of his day, had inspired the poet's pen, though whether Albert Craig the 'Cricket Rhymster' could be considered a poet is doubtful.

Craig, a Yorkshireman who lived in Kennington near the Oval, used to peddle his single sheets of cricketing doggerel round the southern cricket grounds from the 1880s until well into this century. He wrote literally hundreds of rhymes celebrating the events and players of the time, and sold them for a penny a sheet, and when at the Oval used to hide the accumulated coppers in a secret cache at the back of the pavilion before collecting them at the end of the day. Once someone yelled at him: 'Any fool could write this stuff.' 'Yes,' retorted Craig, 'but you can't be a fool to sell it.'

R. ABEL, SURREY
'BOB' ABEL
On his remarkable innings at Lord's in the Middlesex v. Surrey Match, when he scored 151 runs not out.

Tune – 'Annie Rooney'

1 *Patiently our favourite plays,*
 Bowlers change, but still he plays,
 Extra caution he displays,
 Whilst they try to beat him.
 Seven are tried, but still they fail
 To disturb a single bail,
 Tell me, honoured Thoms and Gale,
 Is it wrong to greet him?
  (chorus):
 Well play'd Abel, good boy, Bob,
 You were fairly on the job,
 Your position you maintain,
 Our little favourite is himself again.

2 *For six long and weary hours,*
  Bobby showed rare batting powers;
  'Twas no bed for rosy bowers,
  'Twas a hard day's working
  Still the valiant little chap
  Work'd away without mishap,
  Never seem'd to care a rap,
  Duty never shirking.
        (chorus):

3 *Middlesex are no mean foe,*
  Nottingham will tell you so;
  That proves Abel's pluck and go
  Has not yet diminish'd.
  Bob, your place you still maintain,
  May your judgment never wane,
  Show your matchless form again,
  Ere the season's finish'd.
        (chorus):

Abel's matchless form was not much in evidence in a match that had caused great excitement in cider country. ZUMMERZET VARSUS ZURREY, originally appeared in the *Somerset County Gazette* for Saturday, 22 August 1891. It comprises a dozen verses in West Country dialect, and describes the match at Taunton of the previous week, though whether it ever had a musical accompaniment is difficult to say. The verses are by the author of 'Father O'Flynn' (man of letters, A. P. Graves) and were later reproduced together with photographs of the teams by a local publisher. Zummerzet gained a convincing win over Champion County Zurrey, who boasted a formidable line-up — besides Abel they had Lohmann, Brockwell, W.W. Read, Lockwood, K.J. Key, and their Captain Shuter. Zummerzet were indebted to H.T. Hewett, their professionals Tyler and Nicholls, and bowler Sammy Woods who later in his life enjoyed reciting the verses at smoking concerts in the county.

> *Well, o'course we cheered vor Zummerzet as long*
> *as we could cheer,*
> *And we had our zplendid Zammy, our bowler*
> *wi'out peer,*
> *And our clever Cap'n Hewett and our clinkin*
> *pair of pros,*
> *Not forgettin' a good ringin' cheer vor our*
> *gallant Zurrey voes.*

The starting of 'smoking concerts' in London in the early eighties provided a new platform for many cricket songs. The smoking concerts, with their atmosphere of genial bohemianism, where feasts of the pipe or calumet were held in honour of the spirits, were an extension of smoking-rooms at theatres and helped encourage customers to high-class music who enjoyed a cigar or pipe, and who by attending otherwise would have had to forgo the pleasure. The concerts were male dominated affairs, and gave a chance for lovers of notes plus nicotine to display their ornate pipeware, very much *à la mode* at the time. There was the occasional protest (no doubt supported by the poor singers) from lovers of tunes and not tobacco, who complained that they 'could enjoy a smoking concert very much of it were not for the smoking'. The ladies had their own version of these concerts called 'The Grand Cigarette Concert'.

The smoking concert became an acceptable social activity for any number of cricket clubs, to be followed by the club dance at which the gentlemen would be joined by their ladies. It was on such an occasion that THE SONG OF THE EMERITI was heard first, in honour of the wandering club whose membership is confined to Roman Catholics and whose origin lay in country-house cricket. The Welman family of Norton Manor, Taunton, used to host dances when the club embarked on West Country tours, and it was Captain C. Welman who wrote the words for their song:

> *Hurrah for the days of victory*
> *Hurrah for the festive nights*
> *Hurrah for the blue and black and gold*
> *of the gallant Emerites*

Ettling's CRICKET POLKA, and also that of a member of the Scarborough Cricket Club, R. W. Kohler, who introduced Airs from Auber's opera 'Masaniello', would have been performed at this type of function. Frank Hall's song LIFE IS LIKE A GAME OF CRICKET was sung by Miss Louise Hazelton at a smoking concert. She gave, no doubt, a stirring rendition of:

> *The field's the world in which we wage*
> *The transient warfare of our strife;*
> *Where hand to hand we all engage,*
> *To fight the battle of this life.*

CRICKET POLKA
POUR
PIANO,
PAR
EMILE ETTLING.
Ent. Sta. Hall.
Pr 3/-
London:
ROBERT COCKS & Co NEW BURLINGTON STREET, REGENT STREET, W.
Music Publishers to Her Most Gracious Majesty Queen Victoria, H.R.H. The Prince of Wales, & H.I.M. The Emperor Napoleon, III.

Perhaps the most mouth-watering example of socialising is found in the CRICKETERS' SUPPER SONG:

1. *Then when our game is over,*
   Our supper we will get,
   With good roast beef, some veal and ham
   Likewise some heavy wet!

   Then a stuffing we will go,
   With good roast beef, some veal and ham,
   Likewise some heavy wet!

2. *Then when our supper's over,*
   The cloth it shall be cleared,
   We'll drink a health unto our friends,
   And drink a jovial cheer!

   Then a drinking we will go,
   We'll drink a health unto our friends,
   And drink a jovial cheer!

3. *The pipes upon the table,*
   They look so nice and white,
   The bacca follows after,
   It is our 'eart's' delight.

   Then to smoking we will go,
   The bacca follows after,
   It is our 'eart's' delight.

4. *At last we take a pint pot,*
   We prattle, laugh and sing,
   We drink a health unto our friends,
   And so, God bless the King.

   With a hip, hip, hip, hurrah-a-ha,
   We drink a health unto our friends,
   And so, God bless the King.

The Northamptonshire C.C.C. Annual Dinner in 1885 was held at the Plough Hotel, Northampton. The dinner was notable because of a song specially composed for the occasion by the captain of the club, J. P. Kingston. Kingston had borrowed the tune of 'Bonny Dundee' for his lyrics, and the singer on the night was Charles Thorpe, who made infrequent appearances for Northants.

The feast it is over, let wine cups be spread,
Let mirth and enjoyment run riot instead,
And ye who love pleasure that's manly and true,
Raise your glasses to cricket — so fill up anew.
(chorus):
Then fill up your glasses, and drain them again,
And raise high your voices, and sing out like men;
That cricket long flourish, brave hearts to delight,
Is the wish and the toast of all present to-night.

Here's a toast to our County and New County Ground —
May patrons and players in plenty be found,
To pull well together and pull with a will,
And success in the future our hopes will fulfil.

There be clubs in the country more noted in name,
Whom we hope in the future to rival in fame;
Success, like a goddess, in laurel wreaths crown'd,
Has never on courage or energy frown'd.

In fields more important, and works more revered,
Gaunt Failure, the witch, has no cause to be feared,
If hope be man's pilot and wisdom his guide,
As he toils o'er the waves of life's perilous tide.

THE CRICKETER, a song dedicated to the Cricket Clubs of the United Kingdom by W. J. Bullock, has previously been thought to have been published around 1880. The splendidly coloured lithograph cover with William Clarke, Fuller Pilch, and the Lord's and Oval grounds each occupying a separate corner, surround the singer Maclagan, who makes an imposing centrepiece. The lithographers were J. and W. Pearman of 13, Castle Street East, and the publishers were Weippert and Co. (late Simpson) of 266, Regent Street. Simpson was bought up by Weippert around 1869, and the song is likely to have been produced soon after.

T. Maclagan gave his name to a number of songs in the sixties, BITTER BEER, JOLLY DOGS and EASY COME EASY GO among them. There were at least four editions of THE CRICKETER issued, with the fourth featuring Howard Paul who has his face superimposed in place of

Maclagan's. According to the Harding Collection files at the Bodleian Library, this fourth edition came out *circa* 1875.

The song was obviously popular, and promoted by probably four 'name' singers. It was sung in club bars, in concerts and on stage:

1 *Let others hunt, or fish, or sail*
Afar o'er ocean's foam,
Give me the game that's played among
The sweet green fields of home.
The wickets pitched on a level spot,
Beneath a smiling sky,
No sport for pleasure or for health
With Cricket then can vie.
(chorus):
Then take the bat and the ball in hand,
Let the umpire sing out 'play'
For Cricket is a noble game,
And 'tis our toast to-day.

2 *For peer and peasant, man and boy,*
This game to none can yield,
Both rich and poor delight to show
Their prowess in the field.
Then join your voices, give three cheers
For wicket, bat, and ball;
Success be to our Cricket Club,
Prosperity to all.
    (chorus):
Then take the bat and the ball, etc.

3 *Ye Benedicts, who the 'match have played',*
No doubt you'll say you've won
A darling wife, an angel quite,
If so your part's well done.
But you ye 'single wicket' men
Can't estimate much winnings,
But I hope when you've passed the 'popping crease'
You'll have a successful 'innings'
    (chorus):
Then take the bat and the ball, etc.

Norman Gale was born at Kew, Surrey, in 1862. He lived in Rugby for most of his life, and produced poetry over a period of fifty years. Two volumes on *A Country Muse* were followed by several slim books of cricket songs in the 1890s, and much later. A few of his deft verses have been put to music, some by Joseph Moorat and one by Ellis Wynne. Moorat, who in his early years had used the pseudonym Joseph S. Ward, added piano accompaniments to RUB IT IN; CRICKET ON THE HEARTH; and

THE CRICKETER.
SONG
Dedicated to
THE CRICKET CLUBS
OF THE UNITED KINGDOM
CLARK
FULLER PILCH
SUNG BY
MACLAGAN
LORDS
THE OVAL
WRITTEN AND COMPOSED
By
W. J. BULLOCK

THE CRICKETER.
SONG
Dedicated to
THE CRICKET CLUBS
OF THE UNITED KINGDOM
CLARK
FULLER PILCH
SUNG BY
HOWARD PAUL
LORDS
THE OVAL
WRITTEN AND COMPOSED
By
W. J. BULLOCK

SPARKLING. A rare performance of SPARKLING was given on 1 August 1979, at the Wigmore Hall for Gerald Moore's eightieth birthday concert, when it was sung by the baritone Richard Jackson, with Graham Johnson at the piano.

> *I'm not a good Cover I freely admit,*
> *And I'm not very handy at Point;*
> *I'm growing inert, and no longer exert*
> *The nimble gymnastical joint*
> *I cannot rejoice when a hurricane cut*
> *Confuses my skin with its crunch;*
> *When fielding to hitters my heart patter-pitters,*
> *But trust me to sparkle at lunch:*
>   *I radiate freely at lunch.*

Moorat also set music to another three verses with a cricketing theme, which began:

> *No Spanish Don with a long pedigree,*
> *Or Jacques Bonhomme with his oui! oui! oui!*
> *Nor yet mein Herr from his dear Vaterland*
> *Can boast of a game like our Cricket O!*

Ellis J. Wynne's accompaniment to ADVICE GRATIS by Norman Gale is lively and inventive, but it also contains some rather disturbingly-forced modulatory passages. The dedication is to F. Stanley Jackson (Jacker), Harrow, Cambridge, Yorkshire, and a future captain of England — one of the great personality cricketers.

> *Toss him down a slow you see,*
> *He's sure to have a go, you see,*
> *And ten to one the trick is done*
> *By just a bit of brains you see*
> *But if with equal craft he meets*
> *Your wiles, and does not blench,*
> *If ev'ry bowler in your team*
> *Desires the restful bench*
> *And there he stands, the unsubdued,*

With dauntless front and eye,
Prepared to smack your choicest balls,
To realms unheard of, why —
Don't ask my advice, you see,
No, not at any price, you see;
But ten to one the trick were done
If I were in your team, you see!

Another poet, and also essayist who found great difficulty in not including cricket into all of his writing was E. V. Lucas. A shy, retiring man, who had a hand in over one hundred books, he came from a Quaker family, and was related to Lord Lister who pioneered antiseptics. In 1892 'E.V.' issued five SONGS OF THE BAT, in a pamphlet introduced by the following:

Racket, and Niblick, and
Bladder-filled ball
Bow to the Bat, to the
Monarch of all.

Well over a quarter of a century later, Lucas embarked on a voyage in the Blue Star passenger liner *S.S. Avelona*, and took part in many of the entertainments and games of cricket aboard. He later recalled the time in an extremely scarce booklet *Cricket at Sea*. There could have been a connection between that voyage and the sending of a letter to Lucas that had with it the music manuscript of a song called THE RIGHT CRICKETER. The undated letter was from an A. E. Mortimer of the Training Ship *Mercury* at Hamble, Southampton (the great classical scholar and triple blue C. B. Fry took command of this ship in 1908), and the music was a four-part male voice setting of some verses of Lucas, by Amy Mortimer. Whether A. E. and Amy Mortimer were the same person is not clear, and the music is amateurish and derivative, but the interest lies in the words of Lucas, accompanied by the letter: 'I send a M.S. copy of the music to your verses; it has been to two or three publishers without success, but I shall try again. It was composed for the boys here, and does not sound bad when sung with expression as directed. Should you ever visit this ship, the boys shall sing it to you.'

The cricketer laid his bat aside,
And said goodbye to the fair green sod,
On a starlit summer night he died,
And stood before his God.
'Say what has he done to win my Throne?'
And the Angel made reply
'He preached no word, but he cast no stone,
He spake no lie!'
'But what,' God asked again, 'has he done?
What yoke did he endure?'
'He turned his face with joy to thy sun,
He kept thy Temple pure,
With all his strength, he batted and bowled,
And his heart was the heart of a little child!'
The Angel paused, for his tale was told,
And all that heard it, smiled.

The Australian XI played matches in Australia and New Zealand, in order to raise funds for their tour of Britain in 1878. They also stopped in America and Canada, both before arriving and after leaving England, and took part in a further series of matches on their return to Australia.

Back row, L to R: John Blackham, bank clerk, wicket keeper; Thomas Horan, later became journalist 'Felix of the Australasian'; George Bailey, bank clerk, learned his cricket in Tasmania; John Conway, organiser/manager, played the occasional game; Alec Bannerman, worked in a Government Printing Office, stonewaller; Charles Bannerman, born in England, but lived in Australia from childhood, had scored 165 in the First Test between the 'new enemies'; William Murdoch, solicitor, wicket keeper.
Middle row, seated: David Gregory, captain, the oldest of the team at 32, worked in an audit office.
Front row, squatting, L to R: Fred Spofforth, the 6ft 2in 'Demon' bowler, 764 wickets over the whole tour, in banking; Frank Allen, Civil Servant, the bowler of the century; William Midwinter, the only man to play for both England and Australia and the central figure of a 'row' that brewed after W. G. Grace refused to release him from his commitments with Gloucestershire. Tom Garrett, engaged in the Supreme Court, Sydney; Henry Boyle, Victorian Civil Servant.

The Australian Eleven Galop

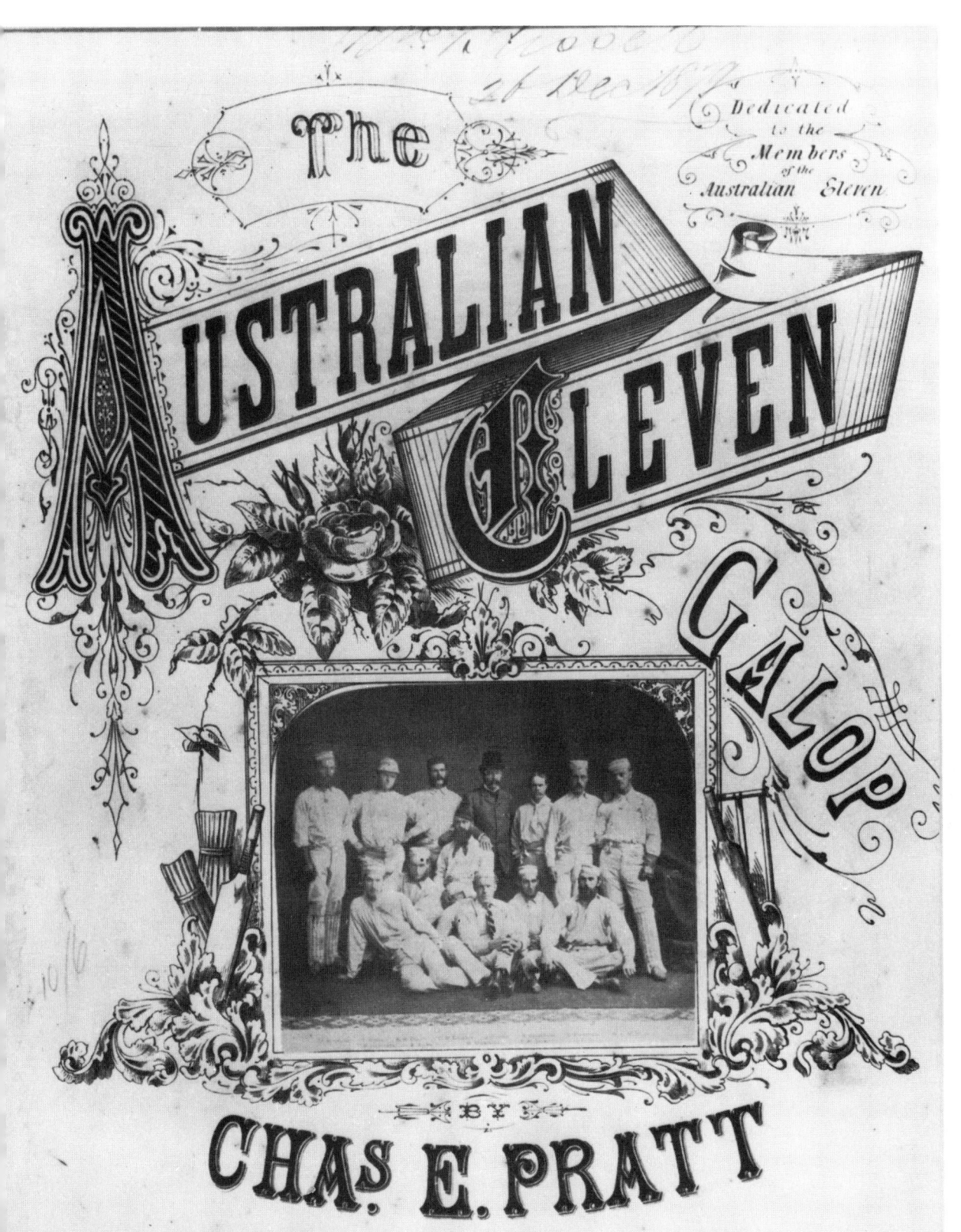

Dedicated to the Members of the Australian Eleven

By **Chas. E. Pratt**

Registered   Price 4/-

MELBOURNE
W. H. GLEN & CO
21 & 23 Collins St East

Pot-Pourri was an 1899 Review that was produced by H. H. Morell's and Frederick Mouillot's Company at the Avenue Theatre in the summer of that year. It was written by James T. Tanner and had lyrics by W. H. Risque and music by Napoleon Lambelet. THE CHORUS OF THE SANDWICH MEN and THE HENLEY BOATING MEN'S CHORUS were deemed to provide insufficient sporting interest; so a topical insertion was made in honour of the tourists of that year.

AUSTRALIAN CRICKETERS' CHORUS

But who are these array'd in white with bat and ball and wicket?
Surely Henley is not quite the sort of place for cricket.
(cricketers)
We've come from the land of the Kangaroo,
Ten thousand miles away,
To show you the best that we can do
At the game we love to play;
For cricket's the game that reigns supreme
On either side of the line,
And we're proud to be an Australian team,
The team of Ninety nine.

'Archie' Maclaren and Joe Darling were opposing captains of their respective forces during the 1899 visit by the Australians to Great Britain, and also for the first three Tests of the 1901/2 tour by England to Australia. Maclaren made three tours of Australia, during which he scored twelve centuries, and averaged over 50. Harry S. Altham, the cricket historian, described Maclaren as being an outstanding reflection of 'the golden age of batting', a high back-lift, a command of strokes all round the wicket, and a general air of proconsular authority.

Darling was a compact and determined left-handed batsman, who played thirty-one games against England between 1894 and 1905. He captained eighteen of these.

SOLDIERS OF THE WILLOW

WORDS BY
GEO. ESSEX EVANS,
MUSIC BY
ALBERTO ZELMAN.

PUBLISHED FOR
THE AUTHOR,
BY
MELBOURNE: **ALLAN & CO.** COLLINS ST.
PROPRIETARY LIMITED.

Play the grand old game once more,
Soldiers of the willow,
While two nations keep the score,
Watching o'er the billows,
Play it true and play it strong
While we crown it with a song
That shall ring the world along
Soldiers of the Willow.

The 1903/4 tour of Australia by England provided the setting for some verses by Mr Lyon to the tune 'Bonnie Dundee'. They follow the time-honoured format of poking fun at the quirks and characteristics of each member of the team, and it is fairly easy to decipher the victims. In case there are any doubts, the side in song order is: P. F. Warner (Capt.), R. E. Foster, B. J. T. Bosanquet, T. W. Hayward, A. F. A. Lilley, J. T. Tyldesley, L. C. Braund, W. Rhodes, G. H. Hirst, E. G. Arnold, A. E. Relf, A. Fielder, H. Strudwick, A. E. Knight.

SONG OF THE ENGLISH CRICKETERS

> *Oh! the steamship 'Orontes' arrived in the bay,*
> *She's travelled some twelve thousand miles, so they say;*
> *But the pick of the passengers, all will agree,*
> *Are the Cricketers bold from the Old Countree.*

(chorus):
> *Oh! it's ho! for the bat, and it's hey! for the ball;*
> *May the 'ashes' come back, is our cry, one and all;*
> *And we'll empty our glasses with thirty times three,*
> *To the Cricketers bold from the Old Countree.*

> *As Commander-in-Chief of this Cricketing Band,*
> *Plum Warner, who's played in well-nigh every land;*
> *He will stay at the wicket, and bat with a will,*
> *When he's fielding, it's certain, he never stands still!*

(chorus):
> *Oh! etc.*

> *Next in order we take the redoubtable 'Tip'*
> *A Prince among batsmen, a champion at 'slip',*
> *And Worcestershire sportsmen all welcome the day*
> *When 'Tip' gets well going with brother 'H.K.'*

(chorus):
> *Oh! etc.*

There's a bowler renowed for his infinite wile,
And possessed of a quite indescribable smile,
If you ask what his name and his country may be,
He will answer 'Ah'm Wilfred! Ah'm Yorkshire
— that's me!'
(chorus):
Oh! etc.

Though in fielding his hand cannot reach to his toes,
The 'rabbits' all know what a bowler is 'Bos';
Lackadaisical action, and break either way,
When he gets a good length he's a terror to play.
(chorus):
Oh! etc.

Then there's gallant Tom Hayward, from old Surrey side,
And all kinds of bowling he's often defied;
He's a pet with the ladies, who cry with a cheer,
When he goes to the wicket, 'Tom looks SUCH a dear!'
(chorus):
Oh! etc.

These are very few balls, be they slow ones or quick,
Which elude the fond grasp of that old 'flower' Dick.
If you play him at 'snooker', well, play him for love!
His hand is as sure with the cue as the glove!
(chorus):
Oh! etc.

Johnny Tyldesley's a wonder, we often repeat,
His batting — perfection! his fielding — a treat!
Though his inches are short, yet his score's always long,
And on shocking bad wickets he always goes strong.
(chorus):
Oh! etc.

WILLS'S CIGARETTES.

T. HAYWARD (SURREY).

There's another from Yorkshire, who tho' broad of beam,
Is the best all-round man in this wonderful team,
And if 'Georgy' goes in when the wicket is 'ploomb',
And makes less than 50, 'by goom, lads, that's room!'
(chorus):
  Oh! etc.

An evening with Len I am sure you'll enjoy;
There's a song that quite fits him — the 'poor blind boy';
And if sometimes he makes hardly any at all
It's his habit of trying to lose every ball.
(chorus):
  Oh! etc.

You must rise very early if wishful to get
The best of Ted Arnold, the Worcestershire pet;
He can bat, he can bowl, and whatever the game,
He will bet you a fiver he wins at the same.
(chorus):
  Oh! etc.

Though the team have left England without 'Charley Fry',
Still Sussex, of course, must a player supply,
And that's 'Bert', who can bowl, who can bat, and can catch;
As a singer of medleys you won't meet his match.
(chorus):
  Oh! etc.

Then there's Fielder, whose name hardly fits him quite right,
So they've christened him 'Soldier', to show he can fight.
You should see Mr Duff when he glances around
And finds his off stump knocked clean out of the ground.
(chorus):
  Oh! etc.

Now if 'Tiger' is weary of standing behind
The 'sticks', very soon a new 'keeper' we'll find;
A Jack-in-the-Box, who keeps jumping around —
That's 'Struddy', who soon will a champion be found.

(chorus):
   Oh! etc.

There remains but one more, and that's Brother Knight,
That wonderful steady and staunch Rechabite;
And since alcohol's barred we will drink ginger ale,
And trust that his centuries never may fail.

(chorus):
   Oh! etc.

There's no greater friend to this Cricketing Band
Than good old Bill Burgess, who lives at The Grand,
He'll dine you and wine you, and do it with zest,
There's no doubt about it, he's one of the best.

(chorus):
   Oh! etc.

WILLS'S CIGARETTES.   WILLS'S CIGARETTES.   WILLS'S CIGARETTES.

L. C. BRAUND (SOMERSET).   A. E. RELF (SUSSEX).   A. FIELDER (KENT).

Alfred D. Taylor (1872-1923) was one of the foremost cricket collectors of his time, with over 4,000 volumes in his library. His authorship concentrated on cricket happenings in his native Sussex, though there were two notable exceptions. They were his splendid *Annals of Lords and History of the M.C.C.*, which was published in 1903, and then even more importantly in 1906 came *The catalogue of cricket literature*, which until the *magnum opus* of the Cricket Society arrived in 1977, was by far the most informative of the three major cricket bibliographies in existence. He was a musician, a bandmaster, and naturally tried to collect anything in the way of music that had a connection with cricket. In mid-July, 1912, he received the following letter:

	Suite 119,
	Maclean Block
Alfred D. Taylor Esq.,	Jasper Ave.
Hove Place, Brighton, Eng.	Edmonton, Alta, Can.
	July 13th 1912

Dear Sir,

I received from Mr Frank H. Casson a short time ago a letter addressed to him by yourself, requesting a copy of a cricket song, sung by myself at our League Concert in March last, at the Corona Hotel here.

I have only one copy, a very much battered one at that, which I picked up second-hand in Gloucester some years ago. Hart and Co., 22 Paternoster Row, London, are the publishers but I expect it is long since out of print. I have, however, managed to get it copied in manuscript, and if this is of any use to you, you are very welcome to it. You will have to suit the words to the music in the first verse as well as you can, as I see they do not follow the original score in quite a few places. However, with a good pianist you may be able to make something of it.

Apologising for the delay in replying to you before I am,

Yours faithfully,
T. H. Clark

The recent Padwick *Bibliography of Cricket* records DOWN WENT THE WICKET as having been composed by Clark, as well as sung by him at the Corona Hotel in Edmonton. Clark's letter points conclusively to the work having come from another hand, and it is in fact the song that is listed in J. W. Goldman's *Bibliography of Cricket* (1937), and is by Rowland Colborn and A. G. Colborn. It is yet another to have a reproduced photograph of W. G. on the front cover, and again its roots lie in Music Hall.

It is extraordinary that a cricketing outpost like Edmonton in Canada should be the stage for two songs on the game in the same year, 1911. The famous songwriter, Harry Von Tilzer composed his equally famous song I WANT A GIRL (thereby succinctly voicing the desires of practically half the populace since the World began) in the same year, and the tune was used by a Mr Sam Walton for THE BOY'S CRICKET SONG which he gave with abandon to the juvenile cricketers of Edmonton.

1 *When quite a lad I always loved,*
  To play the good old game,
  And now it's just the same
  Although I'm almost lame
  I like the game of Cricket.

2 *And I've played it since a boy,*
  A game upon the village green,
  I always did enjoy,
  I've brought my youngsters up the same
  To play this good old English game.

(chorus):
They want to play every Saturday,
The same as their dear old Dad;
It's a manly sport, and the proper sort
For every growing lad.
Hit 'em up my boys and make a run,
Hit 'em hard my lads and have some fun,
We want to play every Saturday,
The same as dear old Dad.

A search for songs on cricket, which can be an enjoyable experience, is liable to end in frustration and fury at a tongue which can have so many linguistic duplications. Let me explain. To go to the British Library and peruse under the heading which could be expected to throw some light, i.e. *Cricket Songs*, can lead one up a mysterious garden path to the Orient. *Cricket Songs. Japanese haiku translated by Harry Behn with pictures selected from*

Sesshu and other Japanese masters. Initial delight at the thought of untrodden ground, before one's 'down to it with a bump'. 'Tis the insect, not the game that is described so graphically. But wait! All is not lost. Another listing in the catalogue. A Natural History Match in Three Innings and a Musical Score by Harry Gifford and Alf J. Lawrance, and set in the syncopated style unmistakeably that of the nineteen teens.

> *Mister Cricket ev'ry ev'ning sat*
> *Gazing upwards at a big brown Bat*
> *And he chirrup'd his love*
> *As she flew up above*
> *But all his loving words fell flat.*
> *'Oh! tell me why does she always pass me by?'*
> *Said the Cricket to the big white Moon*
> *Who made this reply, 'If you persevere and try*
> *You may bowl your maiden over soon.'*

(chorus);
> *'Chirrup, chirrup, chirrup! Oh, I do love you!'*
> *Said the Cricket to the big brown Bat.*
> *'Yes, I do — 'deed I do — Tho' you never seem to notice that.*
> *Chirrup, chirrup, chirrup, if you loved me too*
> *It would be the season's catch.*
> *Let me have my innings, 100 I do want to score,*
> *The Bluebells want to ring our wedding chimes on the moor,*
> *And the fairies wait at the old church door*
> *To see the Cricket Match.'*

The twenties in which the 'gay young things' black bottomed into the small hours, produced the same kind of levity in the cricket weeks that became part of a social scene. Country house matches, and occasional games by amateur touring sides had long been popular; literary, musical and artistic figures, and the trendies of the time, had always enjoyed letting their hair down, and showing an acceptable lack of skill on the playing fields of their maturity. Not that there was not the odd skilled performer. Sir James Barrie, Sir John Squire, and Clifford Bax, brother of Sir Arnold, Master of the King's Musick, had seen to that. Echoes and indeed some members of their sides overlapped — the Allahakbarries with the Invalids and the Old Broughtonians. These sides and several

THE O.B.s BATTLE-SONG · 1924 *

W.R. Vigor

We all arrived in Bath one day at Clifford Vere's call; We thought we were prepared for whatsoever might befall. We had both to trade a rather-gone-to-doubles-class as well, And a pornographic 'Mama' that held Mice in its spell. But when we got to Chippenham to play upon the green We met the fastest bowler-in-ox that there ever was seen; He knocked us wretched stumps about and knocked us well and good. Well, we *did* want to know where we stand, where we stood, Yes, we *did* want to know where we stood......

Now here's to dear old Clifford, the Father of his team,
For everything he takes in hand is sure to go like steam.
The tour may be at Newbury, at Bath, or at Corfe
He picks the place, he gets the men, he gets the matches too.
And when the tour is over, and we to our several ways
They will linger in the memory, these Maid Midsummer days;
And when we've all said 'Thankyou' and 'By heaven this we stand'
You may take it that we know where we stand
                      Where we stand,
You may take it that we know where we stand

* The words of this song represent the composite effort of certain members of the team, who for obvious reasons prefer to remain anonymous. The music is by all the composers who ever lived.

others played their not too serious cricket supported by continuous hospitality. A Bath 'week' for the Old Broughtonians was made unforgettable by the feasting at the bungalow of Mr Cedric Chivers, and their exploits on and off the field were faithfully chronicled by Clifford Bax for the privately circulated volumes that were printed by the Favill Press. The team at various times had included such men as Stacy Aumonier, J. C. Snaith, Arnold Bax, B. W. O'Donnell, Alec Waugh, Harold Monro, Ralph Straus, Jefferson Farjeon, Armstrong Gibbs, and Keith Falkner.

Falkner, later Sir Keith, became Principal of the Royal College of Music, and Armstrong Gibbs, though never a front-rank composer, did have popular success with his waltz 'Dusk'. He had a hit too at one of those Old Broughtonian weeks, as Clifford Bax recalled. 'Who will forget the sensation caused when Armstrong Gibbs and his troupe trolled out the O.B. Song? A song, be it remembered, which had been composed in the pavilion during one of our Lansdown matches, three collaborators producing their verses, and Armstrong composing the music while he waited, ready in his pads, to replace me at the wicket.'

Retrospectively, it seems that anyone around in the nineteen twenties must have been young; not, however, according to Monsieur Lucien Boullemier, who wrote this song for the Trentham Cricket Club in Staffordshire, *circa* 1925.

THE GOOD OLD HAS-BEENS

1 *We are the good old Has-beens,*
As good as good can be,
Tho' getting old and feeble,
Still very good are we.
We're neither young nor handsome,
The girls for us don't crave,
But we shall still play Cricket,
With one foot in the grave.

2 *We can't help missing catches,*
Our eyes are not so good,
But we can make excuses,
Just as we always could.
Our Captain he gets furious,
The Bowler he says things,
But we'll keep playing cricket,
Till we are sprouting wings.

3 *The ground gets further from us,*
    For bending is a strain
    But still we'll play at Cricket,
    With all our might and main.
    Spectators sometimes jeer us,
    And chaffingly remark,
    Play up the good old Has-beens,
    From out of Noah's Ark.

4 *Misfortune sometimes dogs us,*
    The Umpire gives us out;
    He must have been mistaken,
    Of that we have no doubt.
    But we must grin and bear it,
    For many times we know,
    When we stay at the wicket,
    We really ought to go.

5 *We sometimes go on bowling,*
    And strike a rotten patch,
    We keep on missing wickets,
    Our Fielders cannot catch.
    And then to cap our troubles,
    Tho' full of vim and strength,
    There comes a change of bowling,
    Just when we've got our length.

6 *We have some youthful Will-be's,*
    They are a trifle wild,
    And when they play at Cricket,
    They very soon get riled.
    But age and time will tame them.
    For when they're old and grey,
    They'll join the good old Has-beens,
    Who showed them how to play.

7 *Although we're not so active,*
    And speedy as of yore,
    We still can wield the Willow,
    And make a goodly score.
    But sometimes to our sorrow,
    Because we're old and stout,
    We tarry mid the wickets,
    And so we get 'run out'.

8 *Our girth keeps on increasing,*
    'Tis sad but very true,
    And when we're at the wicket,
    Obstructs the Umpire's view.
    But if the ball should strike us,
    Because the sticks we hide,
    He gives us L.B.W.
    Or else declares a wide.

9 *So let us have the chorus,*
    Once more our song we'll sing,
    We are the good old Has-beens,
    Come let your voices ring.
    Tho' some are grey and toothless,
    And some are bald and stout,
    We'll never give up Cricket
    Till time has bowled us out.

10 *The moral of the story,*
    In this our cricket song,
    A man who is a Has-been,
    May be a Has-been long.
    And when we get to Heaven,
    St Peter will exclaim:
    'Pass in the good old Has-beens,
    They've always played the game.'

Indeed they have, however, life goes on (to quote the cliché), and thank goodness so does cricket, regenerating season after season.

1 *Listen! There's a murmur in the downland;*
  Many folk are stirring round about;
  Some are passing southward to the townland;
  They're bringing the old nets out!
  Breezes blow discomfort to the shoulder;
  Early days are fraught with bitter chill;
  Yet the years will find us little older
  And playing the great game still!
(refrain):
  Ah! Fresh Spring days!
  Feet upon the unworn soil!
  All the world is waking;
  Youth is in the making;
  Veterans come gleaming out of winter oil!
  Ah! Great, good game
  Caring not for creed or birth,
  You, by wood and leather,
  Help to bring together
  All good, honest fellows round the great clean earth!

2 *Stiffen'd fingers loosen at the call;*
  Eagle swift as e'er they were at twenty
  To pounce on the hard hit ball
  Look! For life is thronging in the valley,
  Hearten'd by the whisper of the Spring.
  Age and youth are striding to the rally,
  And hark how the old bats ring.
(refrain):
  Ah! Good green turf,
  Rich and soft with sweet soft rain!
  May you find us steady,
  Ranged around and ready
  When our old eleven takes the field again!
  Ah! Great, good game, etc.

3 *Let us breathe the air of open spaces*
  Leave the street of discontent behind;
  Let the season find us in our places;
  The old game calls to our kind!
  Fling distrust and anger to the breezes;
  Here your class and creed must bow and blend,
  Doing as the God of Cricket pleases —
  And all for the same good end!
(refrain):
  Ah! Brave, blithe hearts,
  Fellowship the wide world round!
  Though you may be batting
  Out on Transvaal matting,
  Delhi, Sydney, Auckland, or on English ground
  Ah! Great, good game, etc.

An unashamedly romantic, and idealistic view of cricket that can seem remote from the game of today. The words were penned by Gerard Durani Martineau for his CRICKET SPRING SONG, which was published in 1927, with an undemanding, lyrical piano accompaniment from Edward St Claire. Martineau was born in Lahore in 1897, his Indian-Huguenot name not hinting at descent from the first King of Afghanistan. His family were in the legal profession, and he was sent to school in England, followed by service in the Royal Sussex Regiment, and an eventual career as a schoolmaster, poet and writer. He died in 1976.

Peter Warlock wrote some of the most exquisite songs the English language is likely to possess; indeed they are comparable in quality with many of Hugo Wolf's or Gabriel Fauré's. He also edited literary and musical journals, and wrote widely as a critic, which in part caused him to use the pseudonym of Peter Warlock, instead of his real name Philip Heseltine, when composing music. Warlock suffered from 'irreconcilable divisions in his nature', which led to contrasting moods of deep melancholy and unrestrained high spirits. A bout of the former led him to take his own life in December 1930, almost exactly a year from when this song was first heard. He is buried a few yards away from Julius Caesar, the old Surrey player, at Godalming. It is possible to draw a comparison with the transitionary elements within Warlock and the continually shifting pattern of the accompaniment to THE CRICKETERS OF HAMBLEDON, the unsettled key base between minor and major, the sudden modal modulation to match 'To Small and his companions all who gathered lose or win', and yet every nuance and inflection in the lyric is married superbly with the music; never at any time is there a clash of interest between singer and support, nor sign of strain or jarring note. How sad that the same could not be for Warlock himself. His co-author Bruce Blunt, was a journalist, and a wine buyer for Wheelers.

A note about the match on New Year's Day in 1929, is to be found framed on the wall in 'The Bat and Ball' pub close to Hambledon. It tells how the match was arranged by J. C. Squire and E. Whalley-Tooker at the height of the football season as a protest against increasing encroachment of football into the cricket season. They chose Broad-Halfpenny Down for the encounter, and Bruce Blunt who lived at

Composed for the Hampshire Eskimos' New Year's Day cricket match at Hambledon. 1929.

THE CRICKETERS OF HAMBLEDON

Words by
Bruce Blunt

Peter Warlock

At a moderate pace

I'll make a song of Ham-ble-don, and sing it at "The George". Of balls that flew from Beld-ham's bat like sparks from Fen-nex' forge; The cen-tur-ies of Ayl-ward, and a thou-sand guineas bet, And Sue-ter keep-ing wick-et to the thun-der-bolts of Brett. Then

Chorus:

Copyright 1929, by Augener Ltd.

up with ev'-ry glass and we'll sing a toast in cho-rus: "The crick-et-ers of Ham-ble-don who

played the game be-fore us, The stalwarts of the old-en time who rolled a lone-ly down, And

rit. _____ *a tempo*

made the king of games for men, with Ham-ble-don the crown."

Al - though they sang the nights a-way, their aft-er-noons were spent In beat-ing men of Hert-ford-shire and flogging men of Kent, And when the flow'r of Eng-land fell to Tay-lor and his peers, The fame of Ham-ble-do-ni-ans went ring-ing down the years. Then

Chorus:

up with ev'-ry glass and we'll sing a toast in cho-rus: "The crick-et-ers of Ham-ble-don who played the game be-fore us, The stalwarts of the old-en time who rolled a lone-ly down, And made the king of games for men, with Ham-ble-don the crown."

The sun has left Broad half-pen-ny, and the moon rides o-ver-head; So pass the bot-tle round a-gain for drink-ing to the dead To Small and his com-pan-ions all who gath-ered, lose or win, To take their fill of Ny-ren's best when Ny-ren kept the inn. Then

Chorus:

up with ev'-ry glass and we'll sing a toast in cho-rus: "The crick-et-ers of Ham-ble-don who played the game be-fore us, The stal-warts of the old-en time who rolled a lone-ly down, And made the king of games for men, with Ham-ble-don the crown."

Bramdean, and was picked for the Eskimos, wrote the poem specially for the occasion. Peter Warlock wrote the music for this and another song ('FILL THE CUP PHILIP',) to be roared over mugs of beer by the Hambledon Brass Band and Chorus'.

The cricket itself was not spectacular (Invalids 89 all out, Eskimos 78 all out), but there was the splendid sight of horses and hounds streaming across the field after a fox. The hunt had chosen to meet at 'The Bat and Ball' — unfortunately for them the cricketers had already drunk it dry.

OUR ELEVEN's touring fifteen consisted of W. M. Woodfull (captain); V. Y. Richardson (vice-captain); A. Jackson; A. F. Kippax; S. McCabe; T. M. Wall; A. Fairfax; P. M. Hornibrook; W. M. Ponsford; W. A. Oldfield; C. Walker; C. V. Grimmett; A. Hurwood; K. L. à Beckett; and of course D. Bradman.

A bunch of the boys went sailing away —
To Blighty across the sea
Keeping strong and fit
Each one did his bit
Fighting for Victory.
You all know who I mean
It's the nineteen thirty Aussie team
Our Eleven, they did their best
Our Eleven, to win each Test.
Gee! But how those boys can wield the willow,
Seems as light to them as any feather pillow,
How they can bowl,
How they can bat,
Knock 'em round and never care for this or that.
Our Eleven, they'll be in Heaven
When they're bringing the ASHES home.

The boys all would laugh, when Larwood would 'strafe'
They played 'em and flayed them well,
Way out in the field
They would never yield
Till all the wickets fell
Don knocked up a mighty score,
Even though he heard 'the Lyon's' roar.
Our Eleven, they did their best
Our Eleven, to win each Test
Gee! but how Don Bradman wields the willow
Seems as light to Woodfull as a feather pillow
Grimmett can bowl, Kippax can bat,
Oldfield puts his hand up as he says 'How's that?'
Our Eleven, they'll be in Heaven
When they're bringing the ASHES home.

OUR ELEVEN XI

Words and Music By Jack Lumsdaire

Recorded on
Regal Records G20744
Mastertouch Rolls

D Davis & Co. Ltd

PRICE 2/- NET

Featured in George Marlow's Gorgeous Xmas Pantomime, "Beauty and the Beast," at the Grand Opera House. Produced by Nat Phillips.

Every Day Is A Rainbow Day For Me

Words by JACK LUMSDAINE

Music by DON BRADMAN

COPYRIGHT
PRICE 2/- NET.

D. Davis & Co. Ltd
SYDNEY

In 1930, Bradman was hailed as the 'boy wonder', and on the tour of England he proceeded to make even that soubriquet seem an underestimation, as a triple and two double centuries helped him aggregate 974 runs for the Tests at an average of nearly 140.

> *Who is it that all Australia raves about?*
> *Who has won our very highest praise?*
> *Now is it Amy Johnson, or little Mickey Mouse?*
> *No! It's just a country lad who's bringing down the house*
> *and he's*
> (refrain):
> *Our Don Bradman*
> *And I ask you is he any good*
> *Our Don Bradman*
> *As a batsman he can sure lay on the wood*
> *For when he goes in to bat*
> *He knocks ev'ry record flat*
> *For there isn't anything he cannot do,*
> *Our Don Bradman*
> *Ev'ry Aussie 'dips his lid' to you.*

Allan's, the music publishers of OUR DON BRADMAN, sold 40,000 copies of the sheet music in a few weeks. If that were not enough, Bradman displayed talents in the musical field as well. An adept pianist, he made a record on which the numbers were OLD-FASHIONED LOCKET and OUR BUNGALOW OF DREAMS. He also put music to the words of Jack Lumsdaine who had composed OUR ELEVEN, for a song called EVERY DAY IS A RAINBOW DAY FOR ME (it certainly was during the tour of England), which was featured in George Marlow's Gorgeous Xmas Pantomime 'Beauty and the Beast', at the Grand Opera House, Sydney.

Another cricketing musician, or musicianly cricketer, take your pick, is the Maharaja of Porbandar. The genial Maharaja led the All-Indian team of 1932 that played their first official Test Match at Lord's, although the side was captained on that occasion by C. K. Nayudu. Porbandar was chosen as team leader more for reasons of social status and eminence than ability at cricket. He had a fleet of six Rolls-Royce's strategically placed to convey him to grounds around the country, and several newspapers were unkind enough to point out that he owned more

Rolls-Royce's than runs scored on the trip. He is known to have composed seventy-one tunes of which forty-two were issued in one folio set. The Maharaja explains his choice of tunes for the set in a written introduction: 'As some of them have a touch of the Orient in them, the sending out of these compositions to about forty or forty-five different Countries of which a large majority are of the West, is but a small endeavour to create an understanding and appreciation of the music of the Orient in the West, and of the West in the East.'

The only tune which impinges on the memory is perhaps ORIENTAL MOON, which was published by Boosey and Hawkes about fifty years ago. The majority, some harmonised and orchestrated by Mario Pagliarin and E. Verga, were composed during and just after the Second World War, and have evocative titles like MOONLIT RIPPLES; MIDNIGHT DREAM; SYMPHONY OF THE TREES; THE JASMINE; THE SNAKE-CHARMER; AN ORIENTAL ENSEMBLE; and more inscrutably THE 'ZUMPADI' CONCERTO.

In 1934, there ended a career which statistically seems unlikely to be surpassed, though statistics are incidental in measuring the greatness of Jack Hobbs. Harry Altham's monograph of Hobbs used for *The World of Cricket* says of him that 'in batting technique he bridged in undisputed supremacy what may be termed the classic with the more modern and sophisticated age. Like all great batsmen he sighted the ball very early, and moved into the stroke of his choice with fascinating ease and poise.' To return to a few of the figures, albeit reluctantly, although they are staggering; over 61,000 runs, 197 centuries, and nearly 100 of them scored after the age of 40, in a career spanning 30 seasons.

Hobbs was the embodiment of the highest standards, and most valued principles in the game. The song by P. S. Robinson, issued and dedicated to him in the year of his retirement contains a not inappropriate phrase: *To 'play the game's the thing', so loud in voice let us rejoice, in praise of cricket sing.*

The annual series of BBC Radio 3 programmes from 1975 that concentrated on the songs and verse of cricket, and formed a bridge from the musically esoteric ambience of the minority to the sociable *conversazione* of Test Match commentary for the majority, brought together, not for the

THE Cricketers' Song

"PROPERTY OF B.B.C. VARIETY MUSIC LIBRARY"

Words and Music by P. S. Robinson

Dedicated to

JACK HOBBS

SYLVESTER MUSIC CO., LTD.

6ᵈ

171, WARDOUR STREET, LONDON, W.1

first time, the lyrical talents of John Arlott and those musical sons of the soil, the Yetties. Some of their collaborations are to be found in this book; the one closest to John's heart and which saw at least five different versions was HAROLD GIMBLETT'S HUNDRED.

Gimblett, who was the son of a farmer, was born in Watchet. He was a thrilling opening batsman for Somerset, who once made 310 against Sussex including 37 fours. Inexplicably, he played only two Tests — perhaps selectorial alarm was raised at the frequency with which he hit the opening ball of an innings to the boundary. His debut in 1935 was just as exciting, but let the song tell the story:

> *Bicknoller was his village, Harold Gimblett was his name*
> *Farming was his working day, but cricket was his game.*
> *When he was but twenty, and first played for Somerset*
> *He played the mighty innings that we remember yet.*

(chorus): *Oh, he struck them with skill and he struck them with power,*
> *Times out of number*
> *He gave them Stogumber*
> *And knocked up a century in just on the hour.*

> *Stogumber is the village where Jack White used to live;*
> *But for cricketers in Somerset, that's the name they give*
> *To the fierce cross-batted stroke they will use for ever more,*
> *Swinging it right off the stumps and past long leg for four.*

(chorus): *Oh, he struck them, etc.*

> *Young Gimblett went to Taunton to have a county trial.*
> *John Daniel broke the news to him, they did not like his style.*
> *Then a man cried off, and he was called back to the room*
> *'You'll play for us tomorrow, against Essex down at Frome.'*

(chorus): *Oh, he struck them, etc.*

> *On May the eighteenth, 'thirty-five, at six he left the farm*
> *On the way to catch the bus, his cricket bag under his arm.*
> *Soon to drink pavilion tea, though he felt a little grim,*
> *With cricketers who up till then had been but names to him.*

(chorus): *Oh, he struck them, etc.*

Somerset had Ingle, the two Lees, Frank and Jack,
The famous Farmer White and Arthur Wellard in attack,
For Essex, Pearce, O'Connor, the Smiths, Peter and Ray,
Eastman, Wade and Cutmore, they all were there that day.
(chorus):   *Oh, he struck them, etc.*

There was Nichols of England too, the mighty 'Maurice Nick',
His arms were long, his shoulders wide, his pace was mighty quick.
When Somerset went in to bat, his slips held all the snicks.
The score when Gimblett's turn came round was One-O-Seven for Six.
(chorus):   *Oh, he struck them, etc.*

The crowd had never heard of him, they did not know his name,
But since he was for Somerset they clapped him just the same;
They saw him miss the spin of Smith but very quickly then
For a single pushed off Nichols they clapped him once again.
(chorus):   *Oh, he struck them, etc.*

In with Arthur Wellard, biggest hitter of them all,
Young Gimblett soon outscored him — he was middling the ball.
When Smith tossed up his googly — that ball of mystery —
He landed it Stogumber on top of the old marquee.
(chorus):   *Oh, he struck them, etc.*

Wellard went and Luckes came. Gimblett reached his fifty.
Luckes went, Bill Andrews then played it cool and thrifty.
Nichols took the bright new ball and Gimblett drove him straight,
When he dropped it short he hooked him, and cut him neat and late.
(chorus):   *Oh, he struck them, etc.*

The chilly crowd had watched him while he had changed the game,
And now they felt they knew him and they shouted out his name.
For one fine savage over, Nichols checked his score,
But then the young man cracked him through the old pavilion door.
(chorus):   *Oh, he struck them, etc.*

> *A difficult situation fell on the Frome ground then,*
> *Because the tins there only marked the score up ten by ten.*
> *Of tension in the dressing room, the team could give no sign,*
> *There was no way of telling him his score was ninety-nine.*
> (chorus): *Oh, he struck them,* etc.
>
> *But Nichols bowled and Gimblett then drove him clean for four*
> *He'd done it – scored a century – the crowd let out a roar,*
> *And to this day you may read it, it's in the record book,*
> *An hour and just three minutes is all the time he took.*
> (chorus): *Oh, he struck them,* etc.
>
> *That night, all through Somerset, from Minehead 'cross to Street,*
> *Bristol down to Wellington, they talked of this great feat;*
> *And thousands ever since have claimed that they were there to see*
> *Harold Gimblett, from Bicknoller, make cricket history.*
> (chorus): *Oh, he struck them,* etc.

There were a couple of other instances of cricket and music in tandem, that are perhaps worth mentioning before leaving the Thirties; both with a Kentish connection.

The Dartford Cricket Club were in the habit of playing exchange matches with teams in Germany, and this went on right up until 1939. Any international exchange is a convenient and happy excuse for conviviality of a special nature (not that any is needed), and the visit in 1931 to play Berlin at the Sportsplatz was no exception. The Dartford boys having beaten a weak German XV set about rewording JOHN BROWN'S BODY in a way that would have horrified the composer. The same kind of treatment, of course, has been done before and since, and is an indication of a tune's immortality.

The Blue Mantles Cricket Club at Tunbridge Wells has had a long and distinguished history. Founded in 1862, the unusual choice of name probably originates with members who had played for a private side that was organized by Henry Murray-Lane of Wrotham, who held the office of Bluemantle Pursuivant of Arms at the time of the formation. It is difficult to be certain, as a lot of the Blue Mantles' early records were lost in a fire that had been started by suffragettes in 1913. The pavilion was destroyed, and with it the umbilical link to the past, exactly in the manner of the catastrophic Lord's fire of 1825. The heraldic badge that had been presented to the club by the College of Arms also was lost in this fire, and it took until 1954 for the then Pursuivant of Arms to present a certificate 'granting authority to use his Badge of Office videlicet A Mantle Azure doubled Ermine edged and corded Or during his pleasure'.

The Blue Mantles has boasted members from every walk of cricket and profession, among them Siegfried Sassoon, who achieved a batting average of nineteen for one season, and Arthur Conan Doyle who had a career record in the first class game that is perpetuated in the wicket of W.G.

In 1934, Julian Wright put melody and accompaniment to the words of A. Demain Grange that voice familiar sentiments, and the dedication of THE CRICKETERS SONG was to the Blue Mantles Cricket Club.

> *'Rugger' is grand on a winter's day*
> *When the wind blows strong and keen,*
> *And 'Soccer' is fine and can stir the blood*
> *To a faster beat I ween,*
> *Hockey, Polo, and Badminton,*
> *And some others are good to play,*
> *But the greatest of all is the meadow game*
> *On a long hot summer day.*

The Second World War years make a convenient watershed to pause awhile from the historical progression of songs on cricket, to consider those that fall into specific categories such as School Songs, and the continuous link between theatrical enterprise and the game. Before doing so, however, let us not forget three CRICKET SONGS, by H. W. Timperley, that appeared in an eight-page pamphlet in November, 1941. The pamphlet was designed and printed by Alan Dodson, and contained seven imaginative wood-engravings by Jean Mills. The songs which are simple, straightforward and effective, are THE BEGINNING OF THE SEASON; THE END OF THE SEASON; and SING A SONG OF CRICKETERS.

1 *Sing a song of Cricketers*
Playing in the sun,
Eleven men and two men,
And two who never run;
Playing on a county ground,
Or on a village green,
In summer they are seen.

2 *Sing a song of umpires*
Standing there so still;
One to tell the over
And curb the bowler's will,
One to stare the stumper down
Or make the batsman go,
When either is too slow.

3 *Sing a song of bowlers*
Wily with the ball,
Tossing slow deceivers
That have a spinning fall;
Hurling, swift, and venomous,
The balls that beat the bat,
And then they cry 'How's that?'

4 *Sing a song of batsmen*
Happy in their play;
A week ago a hundred,
And out for none today;
Scoring by a boundary,
Or scampering for one,
In joy the moment's gone.

5 *Sing a song of fieldsmen*
Keeping down the score;
The lone men in the long-field
To race to save the four,
Others crouched around the crease
To catch or merely stop,
And some of them they drop.

6 *Sing a song of cricketers*
Playing in the sun,
Eleven men and two men,
And two who never run:
Playing on a county ground,
Or on a village green,
In summer they are seen.

Verse and lyrics tend to ape their social clime. After the war, never again would be found such innocence, and romantic idealism in cricket song.

―――――――――

The installation of the cricketing creed begins at School, if not before, and obviously the Duke of Wellington's remark about cricket helping on the field of battle had travelled up the Great North Road.

    Sedbergh was founded in 1525, in the reign of Henry VIII, and has a fine cricket tradition. The words are by R. St J. Ainslie, who at one time was Headmaster of Greenbank School, Liverpool, and they are set to music by P. A. Thomas.

CRICKET SONG

Hail to the Name
    Of the brave old game!
Wherever men are English
    and the flag's unfurled
You will there find CRICKET
And the willow and the wicket
And there's not a game to lick it
    In the whole wide world!

CRICKET SONG

If you've England in your veins,
   And can take a little pains,
In the sunny summer weather, when to stay
    indoors is sin,
   If you've got a bit of muscle,
   And enjoy a manly tussle,
Then go and put your flannels on and let the
    fun begin!

CRICKET SONG

Chorus.

And hail to the name
Of the brave old game;
Wherever men are English and the flag's un-
    furled,
You will there find cricket
And the willow and the wicket,
And there's not a game to lick it
    In the whole wide world!

Oh, to give the ball a pat
With an honest-hearted bat,—
Don't talk to me of toying with the sceptre of a
    king!
When friends are met together
With the willow and the leather,
Will you find a better chorus for a cricketer to
    sing,

Chorus: Than hail, &c.

You must leave your honoured self
In the shed, upon the shelf,
Nor think about your average but do your level
    best,

CRICKET SONG

Keep your temper and be jolly,
And away with melancholy,
And shut your mouth and play the game, and never mind the rest!

Chorus: And hail, &c.

— A cut for Six in the Olden time —

Let the lazy talk of luck!
It was persevering pluck
That saved the day at Waterloo and made the winning run,

CRICKET SONG

And the men with most of that'll
Be the men to fight a battle,
For a match is never lost, my boy, until a match
is won.

Chorus: And hail, &c.

So be worthy of your race,
Fellow-countryman of Grace,
And be faithful to the willow as your fathers
were of yore;
For there's nothing in creation
To compare with the sensation
Of dismissing a half-volley to the boundary for
four!

CRICKET SONG

Chorus.

And hail to the name
Of the brave old game;
Wherever men are English and the flag's unfurl'd,
You will there find cricket
And the willow and the wicket,
And there's not a game to lick it
In the whole wide world!

While we are in the Northern Shires, and in order to counteract possible accusations of élitism with the inevitable concentration on the public school, let us turn to a modest establishment for secondary education, namely The Northern Congregational School at Wakefield. On 16 September 1902, they held their Annual Meeting and Distribution of Prizes at the Silcoates Hall in the town. After an opening hymn and prayer, came the Headmaster's Report, to be followed by THE SONG OF THE SEA-KING, the significance of which is obscure at this distance. This had music by W. F. Kelvey, who was probably a tutor operating the strict guidelines prescribed by Dr Ebenezer Prout for those wishing to learn the art of nice noise. Then came the Chairman's Address — Arthur Anderton Esq., C.A., J.P. to boot. The first part of THE PIED PIPER OF HAMELIN, again with music by Kelvey, preceded the distribution of certificates and prizes, and at last, just in case the boys were less than enthralled, there was by special request THE SCHOOL CRICKET SONG, with words by P. J. Wood, and music by, who else, W. F. Kelvey.

When you've buckled on your pads to wield the willow,
Keep your bat in the perpendicular:
Keep your end up: watch the bowling:
Keep the leather ever rolling:
Keep your temper, and we'll shout 'Hurrah, Hurrah!'
Played, sir, played Sir, neatly done!
Cut, sir! That's a pretty one.
That's the way to put 'em through:
Played, Sir! You're a credit to
The N.C.S.C.C.

Are you fielding point or slip or 'in the country',
Keep an ever open eye upon the ball
Keep it fast if once you've got it:
Keep your hands from out your pockets:
Keep the runs down and you'll hear the fellows call
Fielded, Sir, Oh, neatly done!
Caught, Sir! That's a pretty one.
You're the chap to shy 'em true;
Played, Sir! You're a credit to
The N.C.S.C.C.

When you've got 'a pair of spectacles' it's nasty;
Or perhaps an L.B.W.
Leather-hunting may be riling:
Play the game and take it smiling:
Bide a bit: your turn is surely coming too.
Played, Sir, played Sir, neatly done!
Cut, Sir! That's a pretty one.
That's the way to put 'em through:
Played, Sir! You're a credit to
The N.C.S.C.C.
Do you want a certain cure for 'Butter-fingers',
Or for backing when they're bowling at your shins?
Shaky nerves should not be chronic:
Steady practice is the tonic.
Stick to that for all you're worth; you're bound to win.
Tried, Sir! that's a plucky one,
Played, Sir! played, Sir, neatly done.
That's the sort of thing to do,
If you'd be a credit to
The N.C.S.C.C.

It is not hard to decide what the Congregational attitude to *Temperance Songs for Elder Children* would have been. A review in *The Musical Times* for 1 June 1879, on these 'dry' songs by E. Cympson, is perhaps, more objective. 'How old the children for whom these effusions are designed are presumed to be is not stated, but we imagine that it must be before they have arrived at "years of discretion", for, not to dwell upon the unusual manner in which dominant sevenths are allowed to scamper about wherever they please, in the musical portion of the songs, the poetry is scarcely of a nature to train the mind upwards. We pass over the direction, in the cricketing song, to *throw the ball gallant and brave*, because we know that it rhymes with *lave*, but are at once arrested by the four following lines, descriptive of a man imbibing strong drinks:

What makes his limbs look shaky and old?
Champagne and soda, and punch, I'm told;
What makes his coat look threadbare and poor?
Rubbing too much at the public-house door.'

Greville E. Matheson was born in Cambridgeshire in 1859. He was the author of several books (*About Holland* was the one he liked best) and also a prolific lyricist. He provided the words for a number of the *Songs of School Life* that were published by Weekes and Co. in the early years of this century, and several of these had a cricketing theme. His musical partners were James M. Gallatly and Francis Thorns. UP AT LORD'S strikes a chord with every old boy who passed through the Grace gates.

> *Last night I lay a-dreaming, I was batting up at Lord's*
> *And my century was growing fast and furious on the 'Boards',*
> *The Captain of my School I was, as proud as proud could be,*
> *And all the School and half the world were sitting round to see.*
> (chorus):
> *Up at Lord's! Up at Lord's!*
> *With your century a-growing,*
> *Yet another ten a-showing*
> *On the Boards! On the Boards!*
> *To be batting, to be scoring,*
> *Beating records up at Lord's!*
> *Up at Lord's! Up at Lord's!*
>
> *The King and Queen in all their pomp had come to see me play,*
> *And folk were gathered round the ground from near and far away,*
> *From Timbuctoo and Canada, from Skibbereen and Skye,*
> *And Baden Powell and 'Bobs' were there, and 'W.G.' and Fry.*
> (chorus):   *Up at Lord's! Up at Lord's!* etc.
>
> *They tried their bowlers one by one, I carted them about,*
> *I drove them all along the ground, I sent them whizzing out,*
> *I smote their lightning and their lobs, their bowlers fast and slow,*
> *Till members in the 'Pav.' were scared and had to go below!*
> (chorus):   *Up at Lord's! Up at Lord's!* etc.
>
> *They tried their bowlers one by one, their googly man and all,*
> *And one by one they took them off, I went for every ball,*
> *And when I hit a splendid six right into London town,*
> *The King stood up a-cheering me and waved his golden crown.*
> (chorus):   *Up at Lord's! Up at Lord's!* etc.

> *Last night I lay a-dreaming I was batting up at Lord's,*
> *And just as my two hundred runs appeared upon the 'Boards',*
> *With all the school and half the world a-shouting out 'Hooray!'*
> *I woke to think about the duck I'd made but yesterday.*
>
> (chorus):   *Up at Lord's! Up at Lord's!* etc.

The Banstead School Song ON SURREY HILLS, which was the combined effort of J. M. Bastard, headmaster, and Orton Bradley, music master, contains a cricketing verse in which the boys are made to realise that *so long as Banstead hopes to earn a lease of cricket's fame, they have to lustily sing the song, sing it once more, What ho for a halfer! Cart it for four.*

There are other offerings in the School Song series from Florian Pascal and M. C. Gillington, pseudonyms for Joseph Williams, the music publisher, and Mrs G. F. Byron — a descendant of the poet? Their song THE CRICKETER looks to the future. *When I am old and fat, And no more can wield a bat — out in the sun I'll crawl and hear the merry shout, and the laughter ring about, As I sit by the playground Wall.*

The unlikely partnership of du Terreaux and Alberto Randegger (of Anglo-Italian origin) reawakens memories of ROUND-HAND BOWLING

> *There, again*
> *You've smashed a window pane!*
> *However, what's consoling,*
> *'Twas done with round-hand bowling.*

Did they mean round-arm bowling?

There are passing references to the game in both English and Latin in any number of school songs. Vivat Haileyburia!

> *For we've been men and boys together,*
> *Have wielded bat and hunted leather*

Carmen Marburieuse!

> *Vivat vis Pedariorum!*
> *Vivat Undecimvirorum!*
> *Folle, pila, seu tormente,*
> *Civitati propugnanto!*

and a dozen or so 'Old Boy's' songs from Shrewsbury School, which were compiled and mostly sung by the Rev. William A. W. Evans, M.A., to tunes from the Gilbert and Sullivan light operas. He used to make play on the names of 'old boys' who had gone on to represent either Oxford or Cambridge at cricket.

Tonbridge School, which nurtured the other M.C.C. for the cricketing world, Colin Cowdrey, has a cricket song which neatly solves all linguistical problems by mixing a smattering of the 'dead tongue' with a goodly helping of the native.

To cricket we call you, to dare and to do:
Come, comrades all, libros ponamus;
The sunshine is with us, the wicket is true,
And loud rings our Ergo ludamus.
The game of old England, the link with our home,
Wherever we wander wherever we roam,
There rings out this challenge of Albion's sons,
An echoing Ergo ludamus.

Our foemen are sturdy and know not defeat:
Our answer is At videamus!
Their batsmen may triumph o'er all whom they meet,
Still loud is our Ergo ludamus!
O'er Britain's wide Empire, 'neath many a star
Alumni of Tonbridge are scatt'red afar;
And this is the bond that the wand'rers unites,
The thought of our Ergo ludamus!

When doubting one's whisper 'they can't beat that score',
Stout hearts repeat At videamus!
'Their bowling is deadly, we've tried it before':
Still louder our Ergo ludamus!
Old England may stand in sore trouble and need,
When playtime is over, and deed calls for deed:
Then true sons of Tonbridge will answer the call,
Pro patria nos ferianmus!

Stand up to their bowling and play it full fair;
The 'Head' rings with Bene! plaudamus!
Drive, cut it, or place it to long leg or square;
'Well hit' is again our Laudamus.
For doughty deeds done, tho' full many's the name
Inscribed on the roll that is written by Fame,
Alumni of Tonbridge stand high on the list,
Pro patria nos feriamus!

Well fought was the field, we have won it at last;
Come, comrades all, Nunc gaudeamus!
Let Tonbridge be true to the deeds of the past,
And rally to Ergo ludamus!
We've conquer'd in play, and we'll conquer in fight,
The star of old England shall ever shine bright:
Come all sons of Tonbridge, come give with goodwill
A thundering Ergo ludamus!

Uppingham School in Rutland (it always will be Rutland, regardless of the redesignation of a few years ago by the authorities) has always been an educative establishment with its priorities set exactly in the right place. Witness the traumatic upheaval caused by bad drainage in the town, which had many in the school collapsing with high fever, and led to the sudden evacuation to Borth on the Welsh coast in 1876. The reconnaissance party on arrival had immediately explored 'a cricket ground' close to the hotel, or at least a plot of ground to which 'adhered a fading tradition of a match between two local elevens. The pitch was conjecturally identified among some rough hillocks, over the sandy turf of which swept a mild north-wester, "shrill, chill, with flakes of foam", and now and then a driving hailstorm across the shelterless plain.' The meadow was the property of Sir Pryse Pryse of Gogerddan, and with his permission, the first piece of school equipment to arrive on the scene, was the big roller.

The roller soon did its work, and even though technically abroad, the boys were able to sing *Whilst cricket we play each summer day, 'Tis Merry England still*; part of the cricket song that had been composed by the Rev. Edward Thring, who was headmaster from 1853-87, and Herr Christian Reimers who was art master, and assistant music master from 1856-7.

The other song at Uppingham that held great significance with its cricketing heritage was THE OLD BOYS' MATCH. Again the work of the headmaster, this time with the help of another German assistant music master, W. Richter, who was at the school from 1881-6. The words make it clear that the vagaries of the weather were just as much a problem then as now.

> *Jolly Sun, we do implore thee,*
> *Stay with us the whole year round,*
> *Young boys almost do adore thee,*
> *Old boys come to bask before thee,*
> *Lie still on the cricket ground,*
> *Lie still on the cricket ground.*

The Old Boys' Match is the first for which there are records at Uppingham, and for a long time it alone qualified for the privilege of being held over two days as opposed to one. In *Sixty Years of Uppingham Cricket* by William Seeds Patterson, there is an amusing description of an Old Boys' Match in the late eighteen fifties. Apparently the captain of the O.B. team at the time wore apparel that was over twenty years out of date, even though he was still quite a young man. 'He appeared in braces, a broad stock cravat, a sleeved flannel waistcoat, tight cloth trousers strapped down, and the whole surmounted by a tall straw hat.' This archaic picture was gazed upon by players and spectators alike with wonder and delight. He did not come after 1859 — either the clothes refused to expand and could not be replaced, or his bishop's sense of dignity prompted intervention!'

Domum Day at Winchester College is the last day of the summer term, and what better way to celebrate the advent of a long, carefree vacation than to hold a Ball, especially for those boys who were leaving the College for good to seek fame and fortune in the world outside. Mind you, one cricketer from Winchester found not fame, but infamy — if indeed Montague Druitt was Jack the Ripper. The Ball warranted a special Domum Galop that was dedicated to the superannuates of Winchester College by the composer, J. G. Jones, who was a publisher in the High Street. The music cover over the page shows an Alfred Concanen lithograph depicting six cricketers practising, with the college in the background.

THE DOMUM GALOP,
AS PERFORMED AT THE DOMUM BALL, WINCHESTER.

Emily Russell from H. H. R. 1877

COMPOSED AND DEDICATED TO THE
SUPERANNUATES OF WINCHESTER COLLEGE,
BY THEIR MOST OBEDIENT SERVANT
J. G. JONES.

ENT. STA. HALL.   PRICE

PUBLISHED BY J. G. JONES, HIGH STREET, WINCHESTER.

ETON AND WINCHESTER.

A Song of the Eton & Winchester Match.

Words by
R. T. WARNER.

Music by
F. S. KELLY.

ETON:
AT THE COLLEGE PRESS.
1903.

Eton and Winchester.

Words by R. T. WARNER.
Music by F. S. KELLY.

Though It-chen flows a-part from Thames, Our hearts flow to one sea: And rose and li-ly bind their stems In Friend-ship's he-rald-ry: For Win-ton smiled up-on the child When E-ton first a-rose, Who,

ETON AND WINCHESTER.

greater grown, yet calls her own That first of friends and foes. On Upper Club, elm-girded round, Now let the play begin: Let "Flo-re-at E-tona" sound, And may the best side win! To match in lists those

ETON AND WINCHESTER.

Wyke-ham-ists Your wea-pons wise-ly wield, For, sooth, al-though they can-not row, 'Tis said that they can field.

You sons of Wykeham, each a man, Whom Wykeham's manners make, Now score your "cen-tu-ries," if you can, For your five cen-tu-ries'

ETON AND WINCHESTER.

sake! And they who yield on fair New Field— Or be it guest or host— Need not re-sent the strife's e-vent When victors nev-er boast. As light blue sky and dark blue sea Ho-ri-zoned blend their hues, So,

ETON AND WINCHESTER.

light and dark, each year may we In Friend-ship join our blues. Let Chi-val-ry, not Vic-to-ry, Sound loud-est in our ears; For gen-'rous foes give lus-ty blows, But still more lus-ty cheers!

As

ETON AND WINCHESTER.

long as Thames is Thames, as long As Hills look down on Meads, Our hearts shall join in thought and song, Our hands shall vie in deeds! Let but our glance as far ad-vance As back-ward it ex-tends, Down Time's long aisle we'd see them file, E-le-vens ev-er friends!

Winchester's game with Eton was their outstanding fixture of the season. At one time the two schools joined with Harrow for an inter-school week at Lord's, but after that was discontinued, the annual game was played alternately at Eton and Winchester.

F. S. Kelly, who composed the music for the song of the Eton and Winchester match, was one of three highly promising Etonian musicians who lost their lives in the First World War. The others were F. B. Ellis, a pianist and organist with an incomparable knowledge of modern music of the time; he left a valuable library for the music students at Oxford, and also gave a series of orchestral concerts at the Queen's Hall, London, and George Butterworth, who was awarded the Military Cross in the war, and whose haunting RHAPSODY for orchestra, and particularly the song cycle A SHROPSHIRE LAD became so much part of the concerts given by Sir Adrian Boult.

Kelly, a capable oarsman, who won the Diamond Sculls on three occasions, was also a brilliant pianist. His music for the song is based on sound harmonic principles à la Parry and Stanford, and there is a vitality and movement that is never allowed to flag. The words are by R. T. Warner.

As can be seen, this instrumental number is dedicated to Charles Inglis Thornton, the captain of the Eton XI, who later played for Cambridge University, Kent and Middlesex. His reputation was as a devastating hitter, and it was in this match in 1868 that he hit a ball from C. T. Giles over the old Lord's Pavilion. For Gentlemen *v* I Zingari in 1886, he made 107 in twenty-nine hits including eight out of the ground. He seldom wore batting gloves and never pads. Thornton helped inaugurate the Scarborough Festival in 1871.

Incidentally, 1871 was the first of the two years in which the Hon. R. H. Lyttleton of the cricketing brotherhood played for Eton against Harrow at Lord's. Eton won by an innings that year and by six wickets in 1872, which is a convenient cue for that tale of the small girl, a fervent Harrow supporter, who was introduced to Lyttleton many years later after another Eton and Harrow match at Lord's. He told her that he had played against her father in 1872, and that Eton had won. She immediately clenched her fist and gave him a smack on the mouth! Lyttleton accepted the blow without reproach. He knew her parents well, and had no doubt she had been well brought up.

DEDICATED (BY PERMISSION) TO C. I. THORNTON ESRE.
CAPTAIN OF THE ETON ELEVEN. 1868.
ETON & HARROW
VALSE
FLOREAT
ETONA
STET
FORTUNA
DOMUS
BY AN ETON BOY.
ETON, INGALTON & DRAKE.

The Eton Cricket Song, later called CRICKET IS KING when a series of school songs were reissued around 1891, has words by Arthur Campbell Ainger, who proved his diversity by producing two volumes of *Elementary Latin Elegiac Verse,* and writing a descriptive account of the game of 'Fives' for the Badminton books. The music was provided by Joseph Barnby, later Sir Joseph, who had been appointed precentor of Eton in 1875. Earlier in his career he had been a musical advisor to the music publishers, Novello and Co., which no doubt led to the firm publishing two series of school songs during Barnby's time at Eton. Barnby was famous as an organist and composer of church music, and also had an enviable reputation as one of the finest choir trainers in England. He made the Eton College Music Society a highly efficient body, and conducted the choir before Queen Victoria at Windsor in 1889, in a command performance of Stanford's *Revenge*. Five years previously he had conducted the first performance in England of the music to Wagner's *Parsifal*, at a concert performance in the Albert Hall. He left Eton in 1892 to become Principal of the Guildhall School of Music.

> *Though the Muses be silent and History's pages*
> *Disclose not his name nor his date — What of that?*
> *We'll hand on his fame to the uttermost ages,*
> *Who first brought together the ball and the bat.*
> (chorus):
> *You may talk of your tennis, your rackets, and fives,*
> *The skill they demand and the pleasure they bring;*
> *But you're bound to admit in the course of your lives,*
> *They all have their merits but Cricket is King.*

Edward Ernest Bowen was a schoolmaster at Harrow for forty-two years from 1859. Throughout that period he wielded an immense moral influence with the pupils in his charge. G. M. Trevelyan, the historian, writes: 'He held that intellect was only the handmaid of conduct, and that conduct lay almost as much among the small incidents of life as among the great.' This much-loved man was also the organising spirit behind the corporate games of the school — many an evening he could be seen playing football or cricket with the boys right up until the age of 65. He rightly regarded a thorough knowledge of cricket as indispensable for membership of the school, and progress in life, and once set an examination paper on the subject. Question 9 was: 'My partner hits high catch. I judiciously tread on bowler's toes, who misses it; then asks umpire to give me out for doing so. Does he?' Bowen also started the practice of planting a tree by a batsman who had just made his first fifty in a school match. In his younger days he had been an enterprising wicket-keeper who tended to take the bails off before the ball had reached his gloves.

Inevitably his interest in athleticism insinuated his literary output. He brought forth a continuing stream of essays, verses and songs, a number of which revolve on cricket, and many have music by John Farmer, who left his post at the school in 1885 to become organist at Balliol College, Oxford.

The Headmaster at Harrow, Dr H. Montagu Butler, noted that 'it was delightful to see John Farmer's face of joy and mystery when he came to report that another of Bowen's songs, and yet another, was either newly on the anvil or just welded and polished into shape and beauty'. Their wittiest collaboration 'is descriptive of the most lamentable comedy of a certain popular monarch, whose prowess always excites so much enthusiasm among friends, and so much dismay among foes'.

WILLOW THE KING was published by Cassell as one of their series of 'Gaudeamus Songs for Colleges and Schools', and there was sponsorship from Duke & Co., the makers of cricket bats and balls who advertised copies free on application. The dedication is to ex-Harrovians, the Hons. Fred Ponsonby and Robert Grimston, who once took a cab away from Lord's in order to avoid the unbearable tension of a close finish in the Eton and Harrow Match. The song is one of a number that were heard in the public hall at Harrow in June of 1876 at a luncheon given by the Governors in honour of the opening of the new school on the foundation of John Lyon.

Willow the King

HARROW SCHOOL SONG.

No 7.

Edited by JOHN FARMER.

DEDICATED TO

The Hon. R. GRIMSTON,

AND

The Hon. H. PONSONBY

PARKINS & GOTTO OXFORD ST. W

No. 10.

Willow the King.

HARROW CRICKET SONG.

TO THE HON. R. GRIMSTON AND THE HON. F. PONSONBY,
THAN WHOM, EVEN AMONG HARROVIANS, KING WILLOW HAS NO MORE LOYAL FRIENDS,
THIS HUMBLE SONG IS DEDICATED.

Words by E. E. BOWEN.   Music by JOHN FARMER.

Wil-low the King is a mon-arch grand; Three in a row his cour-tiers stand:

Ev-e-ry day when the sun shines bright The doors of his pal-ace are paint-ed white, And

all the com-pa-ny bow their backs To the king, with his col-lar of cob-bler's wax.

Repeat as Chorus.

So ho! so ho! may the cour-tiers sing— Hon-our and life to Wil-low the King!

*** The Words and Music of this Song are Copyright.—J. F.

*** *No 10 from "GAUDEAMUS: SONGS FOR COLLEGES AND SCHOOLS."* By JOHN FARMER.
Published by CASSELL & COMPANY, Limited. *Price* 5s.; *Words only*, 6d.

Willow the King.

WILLOW the King is a monarch grand;
Three in a row his courtiers stand;
Every day when the sun shines bright,
The doors of his palace are painted white,
And all the company bow their backs
To the King with the collar of cobbler's wax.
      So ho! so ho! may the courtiers sing,
      Honour and life to Willow the King!

Willow, King Willow, thy guard hold tight;
Trouble is coming before the night;
Hopping and galloping, short and strong,
Comes the Leathery Duke along;
And down the palaces tumble fast
When once the Leathery Duke gets past.
      So ho! &c.

"Who is this," King Willow he swore,
"Hops like that to a gentleman's door?
"Who's afraid of a Duke like him?
"Fiddledcdee!" says the monarch slim:
"What do you say, my courtiers three?"
And the courtiers all said "Fiddlededee!"
      So ho! &c.

Willow the King stepped forward bold
Three good feet from his castle hold;
Willow the King stepped back so light,
Skirmished gay to the left and right:
But the Duke rushed by with a leap and a fling.
"Bless my soul!" says Willow the King.
      So ho! &c.

Crash the palaces, sad to see;
Crash and tumble the courtiers three!
Each one lays, in his fear and dread,
Down on the grass his respected head;
Each one kicks, as he downward goes,
Up in the air his respected toes.
      So ho! &c.

But the Leathery Duke he jumped so high,
Jumped till he almost touched the sky;
"A fig for King Willow," he boasting said,
"Carry this gentleman off to bed!"
So they carried him off with the courtiers three,
And put him to bed in the green baize tree.
      So ho! &c.

"What of the Duke?" you ask anon,
"Where has his Leathery Highness gone?"
O he is filled with air inside—
Either it's air, or else it's pride—
And he swells and swells as tight as a drum,
And they kick him about till Christmas come.
      So ho! ho! ho! may his courtiers sing,
      Honour and life to Willow the King!

Bowen's verses to A GENTLEMAN'S A-BOWLING, set to music by Eaton Faning, who was Farmer's successor, were dedicated to F. S. Jackson who, with match figures of 11 for 68, had enabled Harrow to win the match at Lord's in 1888 by 156 runs. This time the cab was going towards the ground.

1 *O cabby trot him faster,*
   O hurry engine on!
   Come glory or disaster
   Before the day be done!
   Ten thousand folks are strolling
   And streaming into view,
   A gentleman's a-bowling,
   (More accurately, two).

2 *With changes and with chances*
   The innings come and go,
   Alternating advances
   Of ecstasy and woe;
   For now 'tis all condoling,
   And now — for who can tell?
   A gentleman's a-bowling —
   It yet may all be well.

3 *Light Blue are nimbly fielding,*
   And scarce a hit can pass;
   But those the willows wielding
   Have played on Harrow grass!
   And there's the ball a-rolling,
   And all the people see
   A gentleman's a-bowling,
   And we're a-hitting he!

4 *Ten score to make, or yield her!*
   Shall Eton save the match?
   Bowl, bowler! go it, fielder!
   Catch, wicket-keeper, catch!
   Our vain attempts controlling
   They drive the leather — no!
   A gentleman's a-bowling,
   And down the wickets go.

5 *And now that all is ended,*
   Were I the Queen to-day,
   I'd make a marquis splendid
   Of every one of they!
   And still for their consoling,
   I'll cheer and cheer again
   The gentleman a-bowling,
   And all the other ten!

Eaton Faning orchestrated the song, and it still gets an annual airing at Harrow.

The previous year, 1887, Bowen had written a humorous song, also with music by Faning, which told of the incredible efforts of a batsman to make nine runs from one hit.

He may have been little, or may have been tall,
But his tale is so sad, you will weep for it all,
And it happened along of a bat and a ball!
Boo-hoo!
Of cricketers never a finer,
From Nottinghamshire to China,
But he could never manage a niner!
Boo-hoo! Boo-hoo! Boo-hoo!

(chorus):   *Of Cricketers never, etc.*

He planted his feet — and he lifted his bat —
And his reach you would wonder excessively at:
And the field said 'For nine he will surely hit THAT'.
Boo-hoo!
But they ran and they scampered and fielded,
And such was the work that their zeal did,
That merely an eighter it yielded,
Boo-hoo! Boo-hoo! Boo-hoo!

(chorus):   *Of Cricketers never, etc.*

But he finally struck a magestical blow,
And didn't it, DIDN'T it, DIDN'T it go,
If not for a mile, for a quarter or so!
Boo-hoo!
Oh run, I believe you, he then did,
With speed and celerity splendid,
And stopped with the nine of them ended,
Boo-hoo! Boo-hoo! Boo-hoo!

(chorus):   *Of Cricketers never, etc.*

And just as the niner was done and entire,
He threw himself down to rejoice — (and perspire),
'ONE SHORT,' said the fair and impartial umpire!
Boo-hoo!
So he gave up and went and ate ices,
Of various colours and sizes,
And died of pulmonary phthisis,
Boo-hoo! Boo-hoo! Boo-hoo!

(chorus):   *Of Cricketers never, etc.*

One of Edward Bowen's last school songs composed in 1889, through which there runs a certain wistfulness, is IF TIME IS UP. Again the words had a musical setting by Eaton Faning.

> *If time is up and lesson is due, and youth has got to learn,*
> *I creep to School, if needs must be, and masters soft and stern,*
> *And one will give me good marks, and one will give me bad,*
> *And one will give me nothing at all for all the pains I had;*
> *But good come, bad come, for what you must you can,*
> *And heigh-ho, follow the game, till boy shall grow to man.*
>
> *The worse the time the better the end, and under sky and sun*
> *I go to play the cricketer's part, and turn the bowlers on;*
> *And one will bowl me fast balls, and one will bowl me slow,*
> *And one will bowl me cunning and straight, and then the bails will go;*
> *But fast come, slow come, the grass and winds are free,*
> *And heigh-ho, follow the game, the world is fair for me.*
>
> *They glide, the months of worry and work, of desk and floor and grass,*
> *And till you trust them, fright the soul, and as you trust them, pass;*
> *And one will bring me bright days, and one will bring me dull,*
> *And one will bring me trouble enough, till all the days are full;*
> *But bright come, dull come, they came the same before,*
> *And heigh-ho, follow the game, and shew the way to more.*

Another from the *Gaudeamus Songs for Colleges and Schools* collection of John Farmer's that was mentioned earlier, is SONG OF THE GAMES. It has the distinction of coming from a girls' school at Wycombe, and only the final section of the song concerns cricket.

> *But the summer term is best, for we're out from morn till night,*
> *Then we turn out and play cricket as soon as it is light,*
> *And we lie beneath the beeches when the sun is overhead*
> *Then cricket in the evening till it's time to go to bed.*
>
>   *Slog, run, run again*   *Thus the games at Wycombe flourish*
>   *You're running up the score*   *As the years at Wycombe fly*
>   *Now 'look out for catches*   *And the girls enrolled as seniors*
>   *How's that for leg before?'*   *Find it hard to say goodbye.*

That other temple for feminine form is Roedean, on the Sussex Coast. It cannot be dismissed lightly.

> O, the Cricket 1st XI
> Is the best in all the land
> It's the one above all others
> We admire on every hand.
> May your scores be never failing
> And your bowling ever true
> O, Noble 1st XI
> Here's our best of healths to you
> from Nancy
> Christmas 1954
>
> A verse from the School Song, Roedean
>
> NANCY SPAIN

A verse from the Roedean School Song that was sent together with a decidedly St Trinian flavour coloured drawing from Nancy Spain, as a Christmas present to Noel Coward in 1954.

In all Coward's wonderfully wicked song writing there appears to be only one number that has time to embrace cricket, be it ever so briefly. The revue 'On with the Dance' in 1923, contained a sketch called 'Fête Galante'.

> *Ladies and Gentlemen, there can be no doubt that as a nation we possess many sterling qualities. But there is unfortunately one slight criticism invariably uttered by any foreigner visiting our island. We are accused of taking our pleasures sadly. This to the outside observer must appear to be regrettably true. We feel, therefore,*

that it would be interesting to take a perfectly commonplace institution typical of English country life, such as a vicarage garden party, and treat it in the truly effervescent musical comedy spirit.

(*The Scene is a charming English garden. On the R. is a netted-in tennis court, against which balls bounce occasionally. There is, on the L., a terrace, and then the vicarage itself. The sun is shining and Nature appears really at its best. The only things that slightly mar the general summer radiance are the peculiar and rather drab clothes of the garden party guests.*)

(*When the curtain rises EVERYONE is strolling backwards and forwards and chatting vivaciously. They ALL burst into an enthusiastic Opening Chorus.)*

(OPENING CHORUS)
'RASPBERRY TIME IN RUNCORN'

(chorus):
*When it's raspberry time in Runcorn,
In Runcorn, in Runcorn,
The air is like a draught of wine,
The undertaker cleans his sign,
The Hull express goes off the line,
When it's raspberry time in Runcorn.*
(solo):
The happy-hearted rural Dean —
(chorus):
In Runcorn, in Runcorn —

(solo):
Plays cricket on the village green
(chorus):
In Runcorn, in Runcorn.
(solo):
*And as before the vestry door
With cricket bat he poises,
From far and near you always hear
The most peculiar noises.*
(chorus):
For it's raspberry time, raspberry time, raspberry time in Runcorn.

The theatrical connection with cricket runs parallel with the game's history. In essence the cricket field is a theatre, only one that is in the open air which is where plays were first performed. Whether one sees the ebb and flow of the game as a kind of ballet where the participants perform prescribed movements, or prefers a comparison between the dramatic moment and overall pattern of a play, an actor upstaging another, the supporting players, the entrances and exits is incidental, the two professions after all are meant to entertain.

Many historians have made serious attempts to infer cricketing type innuendos from the lines of Shakespeare. 'I had rather be set quick i' th' earth and bowled to death with turnips' (*Merry Wives*), and 'He's a marvellous good neighbour, faith, and a very good bowler' (*Love's Labours Lost*). Ah well, I don't suppose we shall ever know whether Will Shakespeare was a cricketer.

We do know that Tom D'Urfey, who purged those pills at the beginning of this book, wrote nearly two hundred songs and thirty-two plays — more than any other Restoration dramatist. D'Urfey, of mixed English and French descent, was born in Devon, and often watched games of cricket in Kent. By all accounts he was something of a character, with a very long nose, a deep bass voice, and a ready, impudent wit that was not impaired by a speech impediment that caused him to stutter. He was a sort of court jester, entertaining nobility and royalty for practically four decades. He was often seen arm-in-arm with King Charles II, who, when it came to amusing the assembled gentry, used to lean on D'Urfey's shoulder and sing the songs with him.

D'Urfey's comedy *The Richmond Heiress; or a Woman once in the Right*, played the Theatre Royal, Drury Lane, in 1693. In the fourth act of the play, Mr Bowman sang a song which began 'Of Noble race was Shinkin, thrum, thrum, thrum'. Verse 3 is the relevant one for our purposes:

> *Her* [He] was the Prettiest fellow
> trum, trum, etc.
> *At bandy once and Cricket,*
> *trum,* etc.
> *At Hunting chace or light foot race,*
> *Gads plutt how hur could Prick it.*

This is a slightly different version to that which appeared eventually in the celebrated *Pills*.

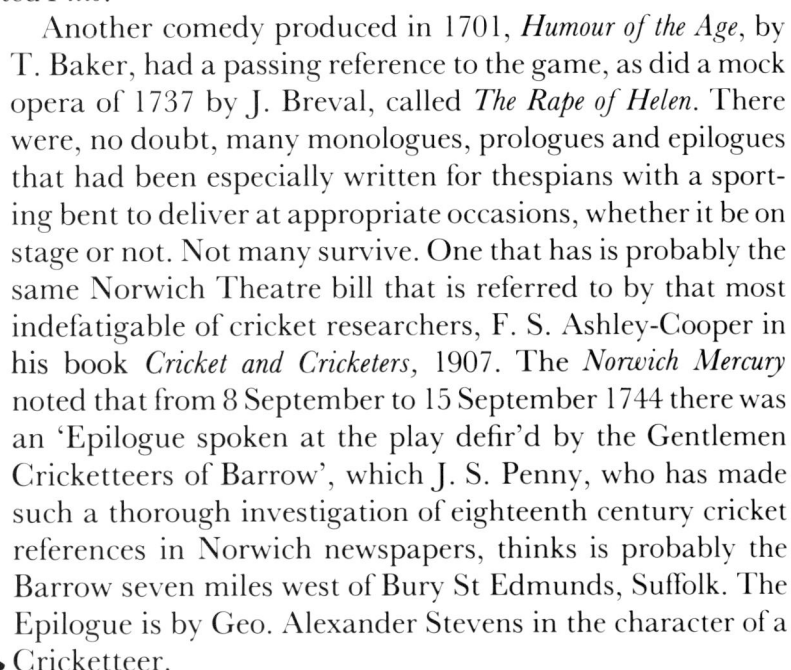

Another comedy produced in 1701, *Humour of the Age*, by T. Baker, had a passing reference to the game, as did a mock opera of 1737 by J. Breval, called *The Rape of Helen*. There were, no doubt, many monologues, prologues and epilogues that had been especially written for thespians with a sporting bent to deliver at appropriate occasions, whether it be on stage or not. Not many survive. One that has is probably the same Norwich Theatre bill that is referred to by that most indefatigable of cricket researchers, F. S. Ashley-Cooper in his book *Cricket and Cricketers,* 1907. The *Norwich Mercury* noted that from 8 September to 15 September 1744 there was an 'Epilogue spoken at the play defir'd by the Gentlemen Cricketteers of Barrow', which J. S. Penny, who has made such a thorough investigation of eighteenth century cricket references in Norwich newspapers, thinks is probably the Barrow seven miles west of Bury St Edmunds, Suffolk. The Epilogue is by Geo. Alexander Stevens in the character of a Cricketteer.

Of all the Joys our Parents did Partake,
From Games Olympic, down to Country Wake;
To one more noble they cou'd ne'er refort
Than CRICKET! CRICKET! ever active Sport.
The Sight how glorious when the Batt we wield,
Drefs'd plainly Elegant, and fpread the Field.
At Diftance wait, to break the Striker's Force,
And catch the mounted Ball, or ftop its Courfe.
So the fharp-fighted Hawk ftoops to the Plain,
Snatches his deftin'd Prey, then foars again.
Or when the careful Bowler ftands prepar'd,
With skilfull Aim, to mock the Battfman Guard,
As Engineers their Batteries prepare,
And the fwift Shot burft thund'ring thro' the Air.
But when the well ftruck Ball rebounds again,
Skims o'er th'unbended Grafs, and whirls along the Plain.

The postscript to the epilogue read: 'Next week will be inferted in this Paper the Cricket Song, by the fame Author.' The song, however, did not find its way into the paper.

Cricket's connection with the theatre and its mummers was in evidence earlier in that year of 1744. James Love, although not yet established on the boards, composed some verses describing the match played between Kent and England on the Artillery Ground, London, which Kent won by one wicket. His verses *Cricket; an Heroic Poem* saw several editions, and have since become an early landmark for cricket bibliophiles. Love, whose real name was Dance, had been educated at Merchant Taylors School (which is a reminder that Merchant Taylors was to be the source of some cricket verses in 1756), and St John's College, Oxford. After becoming bankrupt, he went on the stage, wrote light comedies (is there such a thing as dark or heavy comedy?) and managed a theatre in Edinburgh. Later in his life he joined the staff of the Drury Lane Theatre, and also spent a great deal of money in building a theatre at Richmond in Surrey. He sometimes described himself as a comedian, and certainly the character with which he gained most success was that of Falstaff.

William Smith, sometimes known as 'Gentleman Smith', or 'Smith, the Actor', played three games for Eton against All England at New-

(Positively the Last Night of Mr. and Miss WEST's Engagement.)
For the Benefit of Mr. and Miss WEST.

At the THEATRE, LEEDS,
On MONDAY Evening, June 12, 1780, will be presented a Tragedy, (never acted here) call'd

PHILASTER:
Or, Love lies a Bleeding.

End of Act 1st, a NEW DANCE, call'd
The CRICKETERS, or the Sports of CHAPEL-TOWN.

End of ACT 2d,
The Minuet de la Cour, and a New Alemande,
By Mr and Miss WEST.

End of Act 3d, A New Characteristic Naval Dance, call'd
ALL THROUGH THE DOWNS;
Or, A CRUISE from PORTSMOUTH.

With a perfect Representation of His Majesty's Royal Naval Armament in the Gut of GIBRALTAR, with a Very Grand Perspective View of Admiral Rodney's Fleet, Under Sail, in Pursuit of the Spanish Squadron.
The SCENERY, MACHINERY, and DECORATIONS entirely NEW.

End of Act 4th, A Grand Ballet, call'd
THE MEDLEY.

Running Footman, Mr WEST.
Frenchman, Mr SUETT. | Ben, (the Sailor) Mr COLBY. | Dutch Lady, Miss MILLS
Spaniard, Mr BURGHALL | French Lady, Mrs TYLER. | Nancy Dawson Mrs ACEY
Dutchman, Mr HASKER. | Spanish Lady, Mrs LENG.
Sherpherdess, Miss WEST.

To which will be added (for that Night only) a New Pantomime Entertainment, call'd The

Runaway, or Harlequin's Animation.

(Prepared and Conducted under the Direction of Mr WEST.
Harlequin, Mr CHALMERS,
Timothy Hardhead, (the Clown) Mr WEST,
Colombine, (the Run-away) Miss WEST.
Who, among other Characters, will appear in a Harlequin's Dress,
And will Leap thro' a HAT-BOX Six Feet High.
The Pantomime will conclude with a very grand and exact Representation of The

SEA-FIGHT OFF SCARBOROUGH.

Between PAUL JONES in the Bon Homme Richard, and Capt. PIERSON in the Serapis, the long disputed Superiority between the two Commodores, and the Raking Fore and Aft of the latter by the Alliance, with a just Resemblance of Paul Jones's Ship on Fire —— With the escape of five of his Crew in an open boat to Fyley, and the sinking of Jones's Ship. *To begin a Quarter past Six o'Clock.*

☞ Tickets as usual, and of Mr and Miss West, at Mr. Topham's, opposite the Vicarage, in Kirkgate.

✱ Nothing under FULL PRICE can be taken, on Account of the Variety of Entertainments, and the considerable additional Expences attendant on this Night's Performance.

market in July 1751. England won the first, Eton the second, and England the third. Smith was Mrs Siddon's first Macbeth, though in pantomime his proudest boast was that he had never blackened his face, never played in a farcical knock-about and never ascended through a trap-door.

Smith, like Dance, had been reading at St John's, only it was St John's College, Cambridge, not Oxford. At one time it was thought he would enter the Church, a thought that disappeared for ever when he was sent down from St John's following a drunken brawl.

Whether the new dance called *The Cricketers* (page 133) accompanied choreography on stage, or whether it was simply an instrumental entracte is virtually impossible to say. The sports of Chapeltown in Leeds, of late, recall another tenuous though gruesome link with cricket – one, of course, that is based on supposition. The tragedy *Philaster* had been adapted for stage by George Colman the elder, whose interest in cricket is well documented. His son inherited that affection, or at any rate was not averse to mentioning the game in his plays. The apothecary, Dr Ollapod, in a scene set near Tonbridge in the play *The Poor Gentleman*:

> *Stay — Here's Kent — Fertile in pheasants,*
> *cherries, hops, yeomen, codlings, and cricketers,*

and in the comedy *Heir at Law*, Dick Dowlas, who is articled to a Derbyshire attorney, tells a local yokel, Zekiel Homespun, *I can shoot a wild duck with any lawyer's clerk in the country. I can fling a bar — play at cricket*, Zekiel: *That you can; I used to notch for you, you do know*, and then later in a conversation between Dowlas and Dr Pangloss, who is his tutor.
DICK: *I'll tell you what, Doctor. I'll make you my long-stop at Cricket — you shall draw corks, when I'm President — laugh at my jokes before company — squeeze lemons for punch — cast up the reckoning — and woe betide you, if you don't keep sober enough to see me safe home after a jollification!*
PANGLOSS: *Make me a long-stop, and a squeezer of lemons! Zoundo! This is more fatiguing than walking out with lap-dogs! And are these the qualifications for a tutor, young gentleman?*
DICK: *To be sure they are. 'Tis the way that half the prig parsons who educate us Honourables jump into fat livings.*
PANGLOSS: *'Tis well they jump into something fat, at last, for they must wear all the flesh off their bones in the process.*

Further play references to cricket around the late eighteenth and early nineteenth centuries are to be found in *Fontainbleau, or our Way in France*, and *The Farmer*, both by the Irish playwright John O'Keeffe, *Too Many Cooks* by J. Kenney, and *Speed the Plough*, which was by a member of the M.C.C., Thomas Morton. The second scene of the comedy contains a thinly-veiled verbal battle between Handy, a conceited metropolitan pup, and Ashfield, a knowing old Hampshire farmer:

HANDY: *I say, Farmer, you are a set of jolly fellows here, ain't you?*

ASHFIELD: *Ees, zur, deadly jolly – excepting when we be otherwise, and then we be'ant.*

HANDY: *Play at cricket don't you?*

ASHFIELD: *Ees, zur, we Hampshire lads conceat we can bowl a bit of thereabouts.*

HANDY: *And cudgel too, I suppose?*

ASHFIELD: *Ees, zur, we sometimes break oon another's heads, by way of being agreeable, and the like o' that.*

Master Handy soon receives his come uppance. It would appear that Morton could have been making use of the Hambledon scenario which had passed its zenith some years previously.

In 1815 *The Comic New Year's Budget of Songs*, 'a rich collection of all those now popular and singing at The Royal Theatres and other places of amusement', included THE TREATS OF LONDON, which informed all who needed to know that:

> *There's the Opera House at the West,*
> *A Chalk Farm, and a famous Jews Harp,*
> *Where pay well, you may feast on the best,*
> *Then walk in the Regency Park,*
> *A Lord's Cricket Ground that is new,*
> *With a Tottenham Play-house so gay;*
> *Hyde Park and the Serpentine too,*
> *For men-milliners on a Sunday*
> *Nol de rol* etc.

A playbill of the Theatre Royal, Birmingham, which advertises a performance of *Kenilworth* by Sir Walter Scott, for Monday, 21 June 1841, also notes: 'By Desire and Patronised by the Gentlemen of the Edgbaston, Victoria, and Handsworth Cricket Clubs'. Obviously the members of the Clubs could be presumed arbiters of popular taste.

It was an amateur performance in 1837 at the Red Lion Hotel, Cambridge, which was supported by the leading cricketers of the University that really gave birth to 'The Canterbury Cricket Week', although it was to be four years before the Old Stagers Club was created in Canterbury. The old Cambridge players made the nucleus of a performing troupe that gathered momentum in answer to the growing demand for evening entertainment to support the prestige cricket matches that were being played between Kent and England. That is not to suggest that there had been any shortage of ideas to amuse the distinguished gatherings that had started to become part of the week. Concerts, soirées, suppers, dinners, balls — all joined theatricals as a never-ending round of exhausting but thoroughly enjoyable 'things to do'. Very soon I Zingari were part of the fun, and before long W. Bolland Esq. appeared as Hamlet, and the Hon. F. Ponsonby as Richard III. Ponsonby must have fancied his ability as a thespian, as he doubled up by playing the title role in the most 'excruciating Comic-Operatic-Tragedy that was ever tragedized by any Pastoral Company of Tragical Tragedians': *Othello Travestie*. Othello was described as 'an independent Nigger, but a thought too jealous'. Tom Taylor, who filled the onerous post of Liberal Legal advisor to the committee of the I Zingari Club, made a speciality of writing prologues. On Monday, 1 August 1842, he preceded Colman's comedy *The Poor Gentleman* by appearing on stage dressed in cricketing costume, with a bat in his hand, or rather he was carried on struggling, supposedly, by three men who left him staring at the audience in astonishment. Taylor then spoke in a Kentish dialect:

A Cricketer's Prologue

Hearing they played to-night in the cause of cricket,
I thought I'd come and se 'em — that's the ticket!
    [Producing a ticket for the Play.
But scarcely had I reached the play-house door,
When three chaps rushed upon me, with a roar,
'We've found a prologue!' 'Here, you sir,' says one,
'Just clear your throat, shoulder your bat, and on!'
'On where?' says I. 'Why on the stage, at once!'
And here they've left me, looking like a dunce,
To speak a prologue — Heaven knows what upon.

[*After a pause.*
Well, I suppose I must talk now I'm on.
Cricket's the only thing I know a bit about;
Ten years my shins and knuckles have been hit about!
But, hollo! who are those I see down there?
    [Recognizing the Players in the Pit.

Pilch, Lillywhite, and Fenner — I declare!
How are ye all? Where men like YOU assemble,
It's not a little that shall make me tremble.
While I stand here as champion of cricket,
YOU mind your fielding — I'LL keep up my wicket.
You will stand by me? Never mind my county:
Cricketers are all brothers; such I count ye.
Your cricketer no cogging practice knows,
No trick to favour friends or cripple foes;
His motto still is 'May the best man win,'
Let Sussex boast her TAYLOR, Kent her MYNN.
Your cricketer, right English to the core,
Still loves the man best he has licked before;
Besides, in Kent, what should a cricketer fear;
WICKETS, you know, are PLANTED and grow here;
BATS come up ready made; and BALLS, (just try 'em),
It's quite a pleasure to be RIPPED UP by 'em.
Yet, 'tis a nervous task — for UMPIRES rear
On every side official brows severe —
Enthroned, of course, beyond appeal or doubt,
Whose lightest word may PUT our best man OUT.
Still, tempering duty with good humour, say
TO-NIGHT, at least, that you ADMIRE OUR PLAY;
We'll strive our hardest to keep up the ball,
Make a good DRAW, and with no SLIPS at all;
We promise you that no LONG-STOPS to-night
Shall tire your patience or your gall excite;
And, THOUGH OUR BEST MAN'S ARM BE OUT OF JOINT,
Despite his splints, he'll try and make a POINT.
Then let one voice from boxes, gallery, pit,
Proclaim unanimous, "A SLASHING HIT";

> *And, should we make to-night, the HIT we seek,*
> *Remember that our RUN will last a week.*

This prologue must have enjoyed popularity, as at a later date a Mr Mostyn delivered the same lines to start 'a Fashionable Amateur Performance' at the Brighton Theatre. The performance which was for the benefit of the Sussex Cricket Club, was reported effusively: 'This entertainment which has excited so much interest in the fashionable world since its announcement, took place at our theatre on Wednesday evening, when the house was crowded in every part by a highly fashionable company including the Marquis and Marchioness of Londonderry, the Dowager Countess of Rosse, Lady Suffield, Lady Gardner, Mrs Scott Stonehewer', and so on, and so on, *ad nauseum*, with an endless list of names of whom few had ever heard. The performers consisted of amateurs 'of very superior talent', led by Mr Chas. Taylor 'the flower of the Sussex cricketers', two officers of the Grenadier Guards, Miss Jane Mordaunt, and the aforesaid Bertie Mostyn Esq.

The Theatre Royal, Brighton, played host to another 'fashionable audience' in August 1846, the proceeds going towards the benefit of the veteran cricketer, George Brown. *Lucy Long* was the tune chosen by Mr Hartopp to accompany his lines composed for the occasion. Incidentally, some readers with long memories might consider that *Lucy Long* will never have a better setting than as a bassoon solo, played by the late Archie Camden as a novelty at the Proms.

1 *Come listen all good people,*
   I'll sing you a little song;
   Tis all about big Massa Brown
   Whom you have known so long.
(chorus):

2 *And when he played at cricket*
   And his arms and stumps were strong
   His bowling it was always true
   Although he pitched it strong.
(chorus):

(chorus):
So take your seat tomorrow,
I'm sure you won't be wrong
He's the veteran of Brighton
And the hero of my song.

3 *Full oft a catch he's made at point,*
    In many a bygone match;
    In what he offers you tonight
    His point's to make a catch.
(chorus):

4 *So make this house a bumper,*
    And fill it to the brim;
    He's often made a hit for us,
    Let's make a hit for him.
(chorus):

George Alexander Macfarren, who lived in London for most of his life, composed operas, oratorios, cantatas, orchestral and instrumental music. Though highly popular at the time, most of it is now completely forgotten. During his career he was Principal at the Royal Academy of Music, and Professor of Music at Cambridge. His eyesight was always poor, and eventually he became blind and had to rely on an amanuensis. He was knighted in 1883.

Macfarren composed a CRICKETER'S SONG for the Novello Part-Song Book, and also incorporated a cricket chorus into his three act Opera 'She Stoops to Conquer', which was founded on Goldsmith's comedy, and first performed at the Royal English Opera, Covent Garden. The libretto was by E. Fitzball, and the setting Hardcastle Hall and the neighbouring village in the 1760s. Macfarren scored the village sports for a chorus of sopranos, tenors and basses. The *Illustrated Sporting News* of 20 February 1864, reports that the 'cricket chorus cannot fail to have a first class innings at all future cricket convivial meetings. We expect the opera will be heard by all cricketers round St Paul's.'

Hurrah, Hurrah, for the noble game of cricket,
It strengthens the arm, and sharpens the sight
The man with his bat who can stoutly guard a wicket
Will bowl out the French in a fair stand up fight!

It may be considered surprising that the operatic stage has not seen more cricketing *scena*, even though the Florentine roots are remote from such anglophiliac activity.

The 'Cricket Schism' of 1866 basically was a confrontation between North and South, Yorkshire refusing to play matches against Surrey for fear of prejudiced umpiring, but once animosity engendered invective there was no county safe from the fan, as can be seen when the Notts' Eleven appeared at the Nottingham Theatre in cricket gear in support of some lines spoken by Miss Clara Denvil:

'What means this paper warfare and these spites
Displayed against our Northern players' rights,
This quarrel called by some "The Cricket Schism",
Distasteful term, and in fact a barbarism?
For should not cricket — noble, manly, game —
Be played in friendly rivalry for fame;
And in the field should meet us equals all,
Or peer, or peasant, both the great and small;
But some there be who other feelings stir up,
And one of these I fear is Mr Burrup,
Whose latest insult to our County's team
Is "That a chicken-hearted lot they seem".
When I read that I cried out "Well! I never
Heard it before of them." Now did you ever?

(Scene drawn and Notts. Eleven 'discovered'.)
But here they are, and, for a cowardly crew,
They don't so badly look; George, how d'ye do?
The quantity you've had of Brighton dirt
I'm glad to see has caused no serious hurt;
Now let us, if we can, find out who may be
In the Notts team a "chicken-hearted" baby.
Who can it be? I'm fairly posed. Oh, lor!
It can't be Brampton, Jackson, or Alf. Shaw,
And how you would derisively have laughed
Had I termed funky Oscroft here, or Daft.
They generally show a good account
Of runs well got, and fairish in amount.
Perhaps it's the last edition — J. C. Shaw —
Yet that can scarcely be, for we all saw
Him first appear 'gainst the crack bats of Surrey,
And send them back in a most precious hurry.
Is it Chris Tinley? Does he funk at point?
Time is indeed then getting "out of joint".
Is Bignall he? It did not so appear
When he, with Daft, got off those runs last year.
And surely now (there mere thought turns me giddy)
It cannot be our active chick-a-Biddy.

Whom have we left? Ah, truly, there is Wootton,
Who, about danger, never cares one button;
And with him (ARCADES AMBO) our own Jemmy.
I thought you'd laugh well when I mentioned him — he
Never has failed to make his straight ones felt
When once he'd got his cap within his belt.
No! Grundy's bitterest foe could never say
James ever thought Notts couldn't win the day.
Though last, not least, I turn me now to Parr,
From chicken-heartedness he's very far;
Best in defence as yet, and hitter hard,
I might say more about him only — hush!
I'm fearful, if I did, that George might blush.
One more remark, though, may we, well be seen,
He should be proud of leading such a team.
And let now Surrey bear this point in view,
If they've their Burrup, we've our Johnson too;
So to wind up, pray let us give one cheer
For Mr Johnson and his followers here.'

The Nottinghamshire Club continued to have an intermittent relationship with their theatre. Some years later YE FAMOUS BATTEL OF TRENT BRIDGE, A MOST ANCIENT BALLAD TO YE TUNE OF 'YE BAILIFF'S DAUGHTER OF ISLINGTON', celebrating a notable victory against the Australians, was sung at a charity performance. Then on 16 February 1892, at the Theatre Royal, a benefit was held for George Honey, and the programme read 'Master J. H. Sherwin, the little wonder (aged 9) will sing *It was gone*, accompanied by Miss Nelly Sherwin, son and daughter of the great and only wicket-keeping Sherwin.' According to the paper, Master Sherwin performed 'with surprising *sang-froid* for a youngster'. The following evening Mordecai himself appeared for another benefit performance.

Not all singing reaped such appreciation, as can be seen in an anecdote from Weir and Craig's *Cricket Comicalities and Football Oddities*. Fred Holland had just finished singing one of his soul-stirring ditties when a member of the audience exclaimed: 'Bravo — very fine! His voice is full of timbre'. 'Is it?' queried his friend. 'Perhaps he's been chewing his cricket bat.'

THE CRICKETING SONGS,

As Sung by the Author,

MR. HARRY SYDNEY,

AT

The SURREY CLUB DINNER (BRIDGE-HOUSE HOTEL),
THURSDAY, 15th MAY, 1862;

AND AT

WESTON'S MUSIC HALL, HOLBORN, AT THE BENEFIT TO THE AUSTRALIAN ELEVEN, UNDER THE PATRONAGE OF THE SURREY CLUB, FRIDAY, 16TH MAY, 1862.

PUBLISHED BY THE AUTHOR.

TO BE HAD OF FRED. LILLYWHITE, THE OVAL, KENNINGTON, SURREY.

Entered at Stationers' Hall.] [*Price One Shilling.*

NAPIER, Printer, 26, Seymour-street, Euston-square, N.W.

CRICKETERS' DINNER SONG,

Sung by Mr. HARRY SYDNEY,

At the Surrey Club Dinner, Bridge-House Hotel, Thursday, May 15th, 1862.

As Cricketers all know the feeling,
   Of which I'll endeavour to speak,
When confidence o'er you is stealing,
   You think you are in for a week;
So I feel when singing of Cricket,
   With me 'tis a favorite theme;
But Lockyer may be at the wicket,
   And I be stumped out in a dream.

Your kindness on former occasions,
   Induces a hope that on this,
If I trespass a bit on your patience,
   You'll not think my hitting amiss.
I fancy I can see you watching
   For the points or the slips in the song;
I'm giving good chances for catching,
   While steadily bowling along.

On kindness like yours while relying,
   Who'd not feel a natural pride?
But don't think I mean to be trying
   A "Poetical Cricketer's Guide;"
The title to some might sound novel,
   But I will not rob other folk,
And Fred, who resides in the Oval,
   Is able to bear well the *yoke*.

When the great farewell dinner was given,
   Remember, I sang to you then,
Alluding to all the eleven,
   And the left-handed swipes of Old Ben;
Returns of the play are before ye,
   You'll own that his wonderful fist
Contributed much to their glory—
   His score's at the top of the list.

The first who went over was Tiny,
   'Twas thought he intended to stay;
And Lawrence, that side of the briny,
   Remains to improve them in play.
In safety the others reached Paris;
   But three of the ten had to stop,
For a very cute fellow who there is,
   On the Yorkshireman managed to drop.

From the moment they left till the present,
   Such treatment our Cricketers met,
Each part of the journey was pleasant,
   Too pleasant indeed to forget;
'Twas an old English welcome which greeted
   The players of whom we're so fond,
And kindly indeed were they treated
   By the liberal Spiers and Pond.

One may safely remark of the Surrey,
   Their Club's at the top of the tree,
A team such as their's in a hurry
   We're not very likely to see;
In vain tho' we look near or far, shall
   We seek for a Club with such fame,
Who would not be partial to Marshall
   And Burrup to stir up the game.

Believe me, 'tis not my intention
   To pass over one of the lot;
But some, if their names I don't mention,
   Might think that perhaps I forgot.
Bennett, Iddison, Mortlock, and Sewell,
   Yorkshire Stephenson, Mudie, and Hearne,
Caffyn, Ben, and the Captain, now you will
   Congratulate on their return.

What with nuggets, ovations, addresses,
   (Excuse the queer notion of mine),
None were *stumped*, tho' each player confesses
   That twice he went *over the line*.
Whilst *well in* I'll carry my bat out,
   For fear I should tire the whole field;
To Sydney—I must not leave that out,
   Even such a fine team had to yield.

THE CRICKETERS' A B C.

Sung by Mr. HARRY SYDNEY,

At Weston's Music Hall, Holborn, at the Benefit to the Australian Eleven, under the Patronage of the Surrey Club, Friday, 16th May, 1862.

Unless you possess a Cricketer's guide,
Tho' you might hit right—still you may bowl wide;
But whether or no, if you list to me,
I'll sing you a Cricketing A B C.
    If acquainted with the game you wish to be,
    Begin by studying the A B C.

A's for the All England Australian Eleven,
Who arrived on the Surrey Ground on Monday last, at seven;
B stands for Bennett, who was left behind at Paris,
And Burrup, acknowledged as the best of Secretaries.
    If acquainted with the game, &c.

C stands for Caffyn, the noted Surrey pet,
Whose 79's the highest score that any man did get;
D is for the Difficulty it would be to pick
A better bowler, finer bat, and cover point so quick.
    If acquainted with the game, &c.

E for Edward Stephenson, not easily got out,
A Yorkshireman, and like the rest, he knows his way about;
F did'nt go abroad this time, but met them, and to-night
All present here will know him, 'tis my friend, Fred Lillywhite.
    If acquainted with the game, &c.

G for Griffith, who to get the most runs did contrive,
He heads the list, and Master Billy Caffyn beats by five;
I'm glad to see his *left* all right, Australians will find,
Who never saw his left before, he's left a name behind.
    If acquainted with the game, &c.

H for Hearne and H. H. Stephenson, the Captain, can
You find a better?—*Am I right? or any other man?*
I stands for Iddison, a Cricketer all round,
And gladly will they welcome him upon the Broughton Ground.
    If acquainted with the game, &c

J the Journey taken; K the Kindness which they met;
L for Lawrence, whom they like so well they keep him yet;
M's a letter to which all the Surrey men are partial,
Its for Mudie, for Mortlock, for Miller, and for Marshall.
    If acquainted with the game, &c.

N stands for the Nuggets, quite plentiful they say;
O is for the Oval, so noted for good play;
P for Pond and Partner, who so liberal have been;
All Cricketers are loyal, and Q stands for their Queen.
    If acquainted with the game, &c.

R for their Reception, not forgotten in a hurry;
S stands for Sewell, busy little Tom of Surrey;
T for Tilling, who to meet them, with four greys was so delighted;
And you as Cricketers will know that U's for the United.
    If acquainted with the game, &c.

V is for Victoria, where the match was not played out,
The Eleven think they would have won—but that remains in doubt;
W for Wells, little Tiny means to stay,
It also stands for Walker—all the family can play.
    If acquainted with the game, &c.

W also stands for Weston's, where all the noted come,
Who've won a fight, or gained a cause, as soon as they get home;
The success of his Establishment is certainly immense,
But then he never stops for X, I mean for the *expense*.
    If acquainted with the game, &c.

Y stands for You, and permit me now to mention
Before I go, how much I feel obliged by your attention;
With Z I mean to close the song, for these good men who claim
It, for the Zeal they show and feel in England's greatest game.
    If acquainted with the game, &c.

The game in the United States of America mainly centred on the East, and in the last part of the last century was active in a way that still surprises some. There was a tradition of cricketing families, the Wisters, the Newhalls, the Browns of Germantown, the Scotts of Belmont, and the Thayers of the Merion Club. The Merion Club was formed in 1865, and played on the Wynnewood Ground before eventually taking residence near Haverford College. It is still active thanks to the devoted efforts of a few cricket lovers, one of whom is E. (Tanny) Sargent, the able curator of the invaluable C. C. Morris Library, which is housed at the College. Merion's Club Song, sung to the tune of Heidelberg, begins:

Glorious sounds are the whish and the whack,
Of bat and the Cricket ball.

There are other American songs with a stronger emphasis on cricket, notably AROUND THE FIELD AT HAVERFORD, by Ralph D. Paine, though it was the Manheim Club in Pennsylvania who gathered in the local theatre on the evening of 26 April, 1892, and as a prelude to the theatrical performance which marked the commencement of the cricket season had the following verses recited by the author, Mr Grinnell Willis, who was one of the veteran members of the Club:

A Cricket Song

The cricket is a jolly elf
With a bright and cheerful song,
Who knows that ease and comfort
To an open hearth belong,
When the fire burns the brightest
And the guests are coming in,
When hearts are at their lightest
You may hear the cricket sing.
So let our 'Manheim' cricket
Be the minstrel here tonight,
And sing his song of welcome
In the changing firelight.

Let him tell to us the story
Of heroes bold and true,
Of the boys who won our battle
When cricketers were few,
Of faithful, honest effort
Of treasure freely given,
Of those, who for the good of all
Have long and nobly striven —
Of this fine hall, this castle fair,
This homestead builded well,
The 'Mecca' of all cricketers
Let our 'Manheim Cricket' tell.

In the second half of the last century there were Actors' sides formed to play, for instance, against The Merchants at Lord's. A Thespian Club played regularly in the 1880s. There were cricketing circuses — Treloar's Clown XI, Harry Crovest's Clown XI, Casey and Robson's Clown XI, and Joseph Grimaldi and his Clown's game of Cricket at Astley's Amphitheatre, there were actors such as Sir William Don and Frank Benson, not yet knighted, making up sides with anyone who had walked through the stage door and could hold a bat and then later there was the Bohemians, a private club in Melbourne whose convivial theatrical outings did not preclude 'parting their hair in the middle, and the wearing of clean linen on the field of play'. An ability to sing and dance was the mark of a successful member, and the club's colours gave the name to their song:

THE PRIMROSE AND BLUE
(a carol of Bohemia)

We love to roam away from home,
Life's nought without adventure, boys;
No matter what may be our lot
Our motto's 'Peradventure', boys.

Arthur Sullivan was a member of the 'Old Stagers' (of Canterbury Cricket Week fame) and the popularity and apparent simplicity of the rhythmic $\frac{6}{8}$ to many of his tunes made them an immediate target for potential lyricists. Neither were the words of his partner, W. S. Gilbert, in any way sacrosanct — far from it. The pages of the magazine 'Cricket' are littered with parodies by opportunist writers who were careful to send their apologies. THE VETERAN'S SONG; THE HONORARY COLONEL's SONG; and MARRIED *v* SINGLE, are a few of the many, though it was the Sergeant's Song from the 'The Pirates of Penzance' that attracted the most attention.

Many moons later the same thing was happening, and in the most unlikely of places. The *Chicago Daily News* for 31 May 1939, told an expectant American public that Constable Kenneth Goodwill — distinguished as a linguist, golfer, boxer and cricket player, had served as a traffic policeman in London, and then been assigned to Paris as personal bodyguard to the Duke of Windsor. Surely in Chicago too, such a copper exists without due recognition

When a copper's not engaged in playing cricket,
Or maturing his Icelandic and his Greek,
His ability to give a traffic ticket
Rounds up the cars that play at hide and seek

and so on for two verses.

Gilbert and Sullivan did provide a cricket verse to one of their own songs, without the benefit of outside help. Mr Goldbury's song A WONDERFUL JOY OUR EYES TO BLESS (Utopia, Ltd.) praises the virtues of 'A bright and beautiful English girl'

At cricket, her kin will lose or win —
She and her maids, on grass and clover
Eleven maids out — elveven maids in —
And perhaps an occasional 'maiden over'!

In 1889 came the first of the five annual volumes of *Sportive Snatches* from the Cricket and Football Field, the River, the Billiard Room, the Theatre, and Various Sporting Haunts. Sub-titled 'From Playgrounds and Playhouses' and compiled by Charles Plairre, the issues contained a host of amusing anecdotal material and much whimsy. See the following advertisement:

TO CRICKETERS!!

Rattling good Play; Heavy Scoring.

O U R F L A T

Wickets Pitched at 8.40 p.m.

Ground: S T R A N D T H E A T R E.

In three innings.

First innings — STUMPED
   Second innings — RUN OUT.
      Third innings — Declared Closed, months hence,
         after the BIGGEST SCORE ON RECORD.

The "OUR FLAT" Team

Reginald Sylvester .... Chas. S. Fawcett

Dramatic Author, Steals Long Runs.

Nathaniel Glover	(The Long Stop)	Willie Edocin
Clarence Vane	(Third Man)	Forbes Dawson

Mr McCullum .... W. F. Hawtrey

Reginald's father-in-law, a vigorous Cutter (off with a shilling)

Stout .... W. Heriot

Porter at the Mansions (Wicket Keeper)

Pinchard   Can Hit (at a pinch) Hard   R. Nainby
Foreman .... Albert Sims
Bill .... George Gamble
Joe .... Walter Hales

Employees of the Hire System Furnishing Company.

All Good Changes. Disturbers of the Sticks.

Margery Sylvester   (Full of Point)   May Whitty
Lucy (her sister) .... Georgie Esmond
(An excellent Cover-Point)

Bella	(Short-Leg)	Annie Goward
Madame Volant	(Fast Round)	Laura Sedgwick
Clara Pryout	(Under-Hand)	Alice Vicat
Elise	(Long-Leg)	Maud Graves

UMPIRES:

Boxes, Stalls, Dress-circle, Upper-circle, Pit and Gallery.

Scorers: Everybody.

Nathaniel Glover makes a Hit for 400 and odd performances, and carries his Flat out.

> Stumps Drawn and Carriages ordered at 11 p.m.
> Wednesday and Saturday Half-Day Matches at 2.30.
> Adjournment for Refreshments 5. Play resumed at 8.40.
>
> Admission 1s., 2s., 3s., Reserved Seats, 4s. to £3 3s.
>
> The Groundman can be interviewed at the Box Office of the Theatre from 10 to 6.

A real theatre piece pinched the *persona* of Ranjitsinhji for the character of the Indian Prince who played cricket rather well. *The Great Ruby* was produced at Drury Lane in 1898, and included a scene set at Lord's, though that is not where the missing jewel was found. Six years earlier J. M. Barrie's play, *Walker London,* had done the same sort of thing with Grace.

Cricket's comedic possibilities were fully explored by Music Hall. The game provided a constant source of material for 'business', joke and patter. *Our Club's called the 'Jossers', we're all married men — Oh, it's a splendid game — to look at — we played our first match today — Tradesmen versus Policemen — I was the only sober man on the field, but what upset me was some fellows playing close to us, their ball came flying over to us — I stopp'd it — with my waistcoat— third button — the fools sang out "Thank you, sir, thank you, sir", I didn't want to quarrel so I merely said "Welcome, don't mention it", and then my missus swore she heard me say I'd got two "Maidens" and one "Over". I haven't been home since!*

Part of Herbert Campbell's patter when singing THE JOSSERS' CRICKET CLUB. 'Josser' was apparently the term used to denote 'a bit of a fool', and the comedian Mark Sheridan, who became synonymous with **I DO LIKE TO BE BESIDE THE SEASIDE, and WHO WERE YOU WITH LAST NIGHT,** used the word for his song relating 'the true story of a Test Match'

> *Good evening, friends! Of course you all know me*
> *I'm the greatest cricketer you ever did see,*
> *When Warner saw me his face did beam;*
> *He said: 'I'll put you up for the Australian team'.*
> *They sent a committee down to see me play;*
> *When they saw me they began to shout 'Hooray',*
> *They said, 'In his method of attack there's "Grace",*
> *He's a wonder with the willow, we can see it in his face.'*

Naturally after securing Sheridan's services with a mere 'hundred in the bank, freehold house, and acres galore', he befell every possible, and several impossible misadventures during the match and finished the song with

> *The moral of the story that I'm singing here tonight*
> *Is, Football's not the only game that's finished with a fight,*
> *And if any further information you require*
> *Take my word upon it, for believe me, I'm a liar.*

Sheridan's stage costume was tall bowler, and tight bell-bottom trousers with wide flare. Like so many comics, he tended to be a morose individual off stage, and after a particularly hostile reception in Glasgow (the graveyard of so many funny men), he went into a public park and shot himself.

The character vocalist Charles Coborn interpolated a cricketing verse into I'M RATHER TOO OLD FOR IT NOW; and Fred Harvey sang OUT, which included a verse and chorus on the game that finished with

> *I turned my back and saw it was the wicket-keeper's jaw*
> *That I'd clouted with my bat, and knocked it in.*

Fred Frampton composed and sang a humorous song called THE CRICKET-MAN, which could have started the suffragette movement. It pokes fun at the usual male/female relationships — wife, daughter, mistress, ma-in-law, with each verse containing three cricketing clichés as punch lines; probably in the Halls they were shouted by the audience.

> *Now you teach a girl to ride a bike and she runs into a wall*
> *Maiden over.*
> *Of course you rush to help her and to save her from a fall*
> *Well caught Sir!*
> *Then you find the bike is damaged, but she says oh never mind*
> *You wheel it to a cycle shop and she thinks you are too kind,*
> *But she lets you pay the bill for her, when you get outside you find*
> *You're stumped!*

My Cricket Girl

It's another tale of love altho' it's not about a loon;
I'll promise you no honey and I'll promise you no moon
I see my little lady nearly every afternoon;
I'll tell you how we first made friends.
It was in July, the cricket season
She was there to see our club boys play;
When she caught my eye, I won't deny,
I scored no more that day.
Now ev'ry time a match is played,
In the crowd you'll find that maid.

(chorus):   *She is my cricketing girl*   *I'll make a match of my own*
                My love, my queen!   *With this sweet pearl;*
                Each day, to watch the play,   *I mean to make a long stop*
                Upon the field, she is seen   *With my cricket girl.*

Now perhaps 'twas egotistic, but I fancied I could see
The object of her visits to the cricket ground was me,
So ventured to invite her the next afternoon to tea,
And that is where our match was made.
On resuming play, I took my innings,
And my lady's promise brought me luck;
Though she made me score a great deal more,
Yet I call her my duck.
The other boys want her, no doubt
But I've bowled the whole lot out.

Now, I meet her ev'ry Knight, for that's the time the bats come out;
They're jealous 'cos I'm Abel now to Trott this girl about;
But then I Hearne the right, for there is not the slightest doubt
Her father quite agrees I should
For he says he'll hand this maiden over
And the smaller Fry will Read one day,
That this queen of Grace will take her place
In wedlock, I daresay.
And then 'tis, I, of course, you see,
Of this Lockwood hold the Key.

This song must not be sung in theatres or Music Halls, without permission.
ALSO SUNG BY CLIFTON BARRITT & WILL. E. EDWARDS.
THE CRICKET-MAN.
HUMOROUS SONG.
"BOWLED OUT"
DADDY
MY WIFE
SHE RUNS INTO A WALL
"MAIDEN OVER"
"BAIL WANTED"
Written, Composed & Sung by
FRED FRAMPTON.
Fred Frampton
Copyright 1904. by Keith. Prowse & Co Ld
Price 4/-
London
KEITH, PROWSE & Co Ltd 48, CHEAPSIDE, E.C.
Publishing Depôt 42, Poland St W.

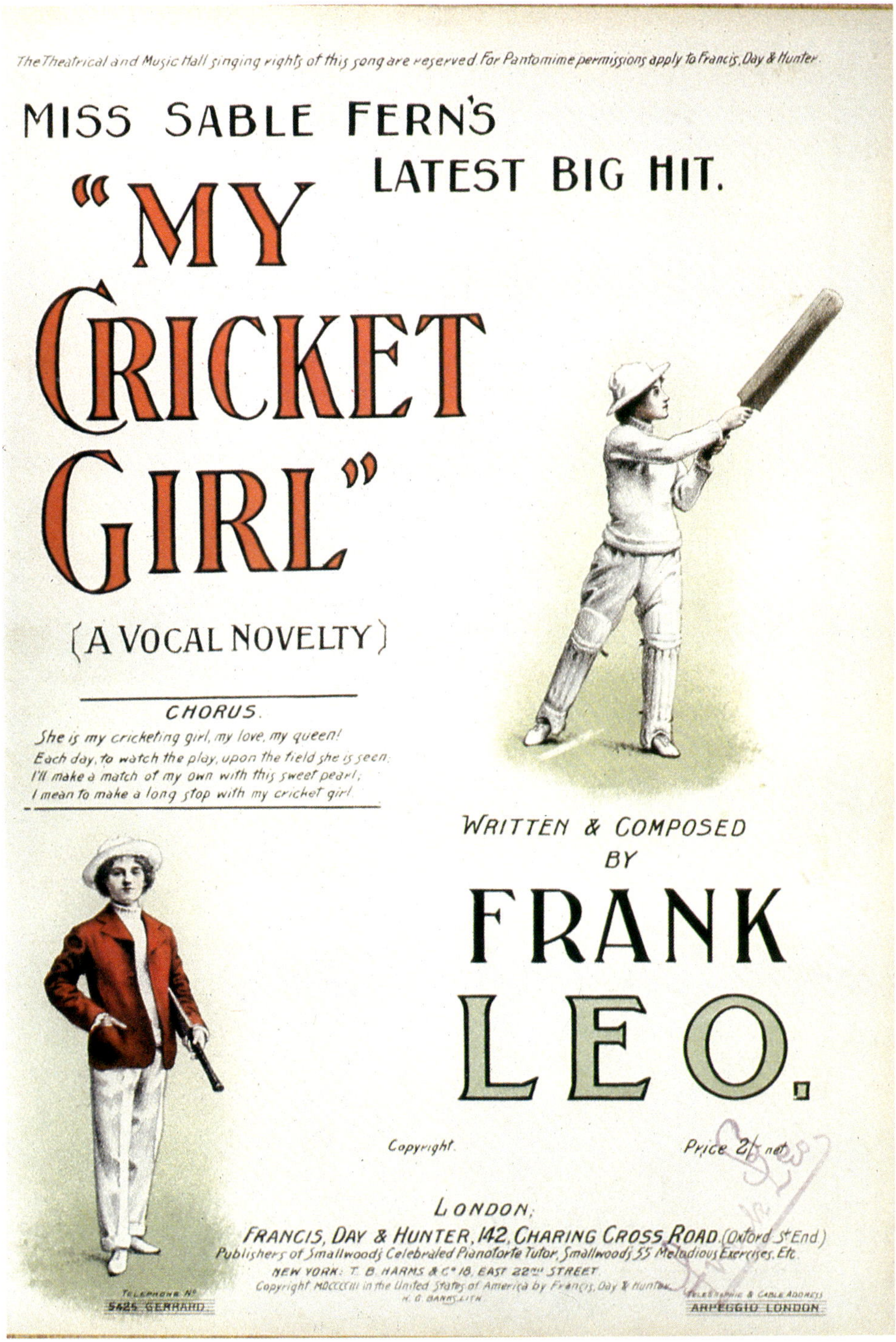
The Theatrical and Music Hall singing rights of this song are reserved. For Pantomime permissions apply to Francis, Day & Hunter.
MISS SABLE FERN'S
LATEST BIG HIT.
"MY CRICKET GIRL"
(A VOCAL NOVELTY)
CHORUS.
She is my cricketing girl, my love, my queen!
Each day, to watch the play, upon the field she is seen;
I'll make a match of my own with this sweet pearl;
I mean to make a long stop with my cricket girl.
WRITTEN & COMPOSED BY
FRANK LEO.
Copyright.
Price 2/- net
LONDON;
FRANCIS, DAY & HUNTER, 142, CHARING CROSS ROAD. (Oxford St End)
Publishers of Smallwood's Celebrated Pianoforte Tutor, Smallwood's 55 Melodious Exercises, Etc.
NEW YORK: T. B. HARMS & Co 18, EAST 22nd STREET.
Copyright MDCCCCIII in the United States of America by Francis, Day & Hunter.
H. G. BANKS, LITH.
TELEPHONE No
5425 GERRARD.
TELEGRAPHIC & CABLE ADDRESS
ARPEGGIO LONDON.

The romantic liaison of the song actually found a parallel with the composer and his singer. Sable Fern and Frank Leo conducted an affair that created a scandal. Her husband had learnt of their assignations, made an unsuccessful attempt to kill both of them, and then turned the gun on himself. After this managements tended to ostracise the lady for a while although she did make a successful comeback, and carried on living with Leo. It is generally thought they married in July of 1905.

There is a story of how she was contracted to appear as a cowboy for a show at the London Coliseum. The director required her to make an entrance on a horse, so he sent her down to some stables at Mortlake to have a few riding lessons. On arriving at the stables, Miss Fern confidently mounted the mare, dressed in fur coat, hat and *cricket trousers*, and then started to practise her song. This was too much for the horse. It took off at a great rate of knots down Mortlake High Street with Sable Fern hanging on for dear life!

Cricket terminology tends to dictate suitable titles for songs on the subject, immediate identification being only one of the advantages, and certainly the cry 'How's That?' has been used with effect more than once. Robert Brooke, editor of the Association of Cricket Statisticians, had relatives who performed a Music Hall ditty with the same questioning title plus the answer.

HOW'S THAT? – WELL CAUGHT!

Once I thought I'd like to be a cricketer,
so into the Park I took a gentle stroll
Saw a cricket match, the first one in my 'natch',
Tried to learn the proper way to bowl.
One man there, he knew how to bat a bit,
knocked one ball, right up in the air,
wonderfully high, looked like sticking to the sky
I stood watching it right above my head,
Come away from under it, everybody said,
but I knew how to catch it, all about it I had read,
in a little penny book I'd bought.
My eyes were shut, my mouth was open wide,
I felt a kind of earthquake, I thought I should have died
but they never got that ball again from out of my inside
How's that? – Well caught!

There are striking similarities between this song and the first verse and chorus of HOW'S THAT? by Worton David and Shirley Ilton

> *In a cricket match I was picked to play,*
> *In a flannel shirt I looked very pert,*
> *The captain said 'Come here, drop dead*
> *You'll field long field to-day.*
> *A ball was struck and it went so high*
> *That it knocked some blue wash off the sky,*
> *I opened my mouth, when it dropp'd right in,*
> *And a chap to the umpire said with a grin*

(chorus):
> *How's that? he said, out,*
> *He's caught it he was right*
> *But I replied it's not out though,*
> *I've swallowed that ball if you want to know,*
> *You call yourself an umpire?*
> *Tush, tush, you make me grin*
> *Why that ball's inside my — anyhow,*
> *How can it be out when it's in?*

T. E. Dunville, who was billed as an eccentric comedian, and whose real name was Thomas Edward Wallen, had an eventful start on the stage in Barnsley. He and a partner used to perform a high-kicking and legmania act, and on the opening night of the engagement all the carefully worked-out tricks went wrong. Dunville's high kicks which were meant to swing over his partner's head instead hit his ears, which was not conducive towards a good working relationship. Then in the Finale they both stuck inside barrels, and had to be wheeled off by stagehands. Nevertheless, the unintentional comedy was a great success, and the manager of the theatre prolonged their stay.

Dunville was another Music Hall artist who found a sticky end. Maybe the reasons for this are not hard to find. After the First World War the Music Hall was undergoing change, and engagements became harder to find; some could only foresee a gloomy future. For Dunville, then in his fifties, it may have seemed that the only solution was to drown himself at Caversham Lock, near Reading.

A couple of decades earlier he must have been in a very different frame

Theatre, and Music Hall Rights Reserved.

REEDER & WALSH'S SIXPENNY MUSICAL MARVELS.

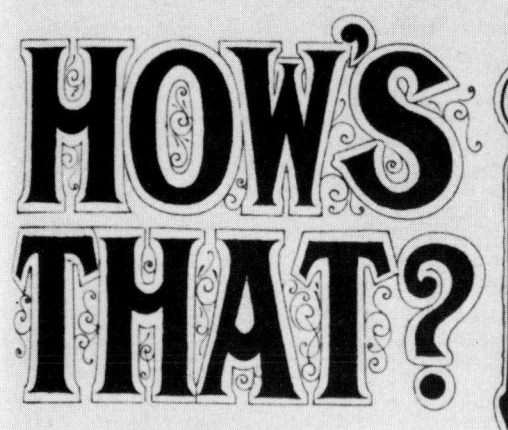

HOW'S THAT?

CHORUS
"How's that" he said "out"
He's caught it, he was right
But I replied, it's not out, though
I've swallowed that ball if you want to know
You call yourself an umpire?
Tush, Tush, you make me grin
Why, that ball's inside my — anyhow
How can it be out, when it's in?

WRITTEN BY
WORTON DAVID
COMPOSED BY
SHIRLEY ILTON

Sung by
T. E. DUNVILLE

Copyright.

REEDER & WALSH.
14, CASTLE STREET, LONDON, W.

Copyright MCMVI by Reeder & Walsh. International copyright secured.

45 REEDER & WALSH'S LATEST COMIC ANNUAL CONTAINS 16 POPULAR SONGS PRICE 1/- NET

of mind as one of the Music Hall Artists' team that played a charity match against the Old English at the Oval. The 'official scorecard' makes remarkable reading, and it was reported that the 'celebrated Dan Leno was out in almost every way that was possible before he was induced to retire to the shelter of the pavilion'.

Music Hall Artists' Team

Dan Leno, kicked out	999
J. Edmunds, can't stop, gone to sell match cards	0
T. McNaughton, carried out	130
J. Edmunds, shot out	10
W. Cobbett, running out	20
F. NcNaughton, slung out	7
W. Alberts, gone to football match	0
F. Glenister, called home, wife ill	600
Stebb and Trepp, fell over step	101
Alf. Sager, gone to nest	1
Alf. O'Nester, bowled 'Charley's Aunt'	050
A. Tressider, gone hopping	201
Fred Griffiths, out for picking up bails	45
C. Phydora, gone away with the fever	007
T. Calloway, leg behind wicket, bowled Kingsland	15
Able and Welsh, arrested P.S. No. 1 L	001
W. Evans, tumbled out	19
Bob Hutt, rejected	50
T. E. Dunville, caught 'Special Irish'	1-6
H. Tate, assaulted umpire	00
F. W. Moss, retired for refreshments	000
Bros. Poluskis, hit wicket-keeper	13
Bruce Smith, still running	0
Willie Bassett, went to sleep	97
Bros. Egberts, rolled out	1
Tatem. Bilious, b Hayes	3
Percy Perman, unwell, b Lockwood	36
Willie Perman, caught by mistake	40
Total	250

.NNINGTON OVAL.

By kind permission S.C.C.C.

LOOK OUT FOR THE
5th SEPTEMBER, 1901.

THE GREAT
COMIC CRICKET
MATCH.

FOR THE BENEFIT OF THE FOLLOWING INSTITUTIONS:
MUSIC HALL BENEVOLENT FUND. LICENSED VICTUALLERS SCHOOLS, Kennington Lane. NEW BELGRAVE HOSPITAL for CHILDREN, Clapham Rd.

DAN LENO,
Captains the Music Hall Artist's Team,

AND

T. R. DEWAR, M.P.
the Old English Team.

BANDS OF THE
ROYAL IRISH GUARDS,
"L" DIVISION OF POLICE,
AND BOYS OF THE
LICENSED VICTUALLERS SCHOOL
WILL ATTEND.

VARIETY SIDE SHOWS
By the Leading Music Hall Artists.

ADMISSION 6d.
Gates Open at 11 a.m.

Halsop & Co., Printers, 11, Ludgate Hill, E.C.

Old English Team

T. R. Dewar, retired to rest 0
F. Turner, thrown out, bowled Dan Leno 0
S. Casey, caught by one of the crowd 0
G. Park, gone to borrow a bob 0
G. Tremmer, obstructing field 0
R. C. Brisley, forced out 0
Carlo, got the mumps 0
W. Mott, afraid to go in 0
F. Cates, insulting the umpire 0
F. Stedman, exhausted 0
W. Lees, caught Leno, bowled J. Edmunds 0
E. Hayes, bowled Hutt all over the shop 0
D. Kingsland, sent away 0
W. Lockwood, ordered away 0
              Total 0

There is no doubt that C. Phydora went away with fever to protect his identity as a well-known secret agent!

In the same year as that match, 1901, and about three miles north across the Thames, Mr Tom B. Davis was directing a production at the Lyric Theatre of a modern extravaganza called THE SILVER SLIPPER, which had words provided by George Rollit, and the dubiously named W. H. Risque, and music by Leslie Stuart. The unlikely settings included the Courts of Justice on the Planet Venus, Neuilly Fair, and the Turkey Room in the Art Club, Paris. That did not stop the audience, however, learning about 'a little lady who was nearly seventeen and pretended to be clever, who was taken to see the "Varsity Match at Lord's, said too much in an accent very strange, and scratched a fellow's patent boots by playing "footy-footy".' SHE DIDN'T KNOW ENOUGH ABOUT THE GAME, was the title of the song, which was sung by Louis Bradfield. Which game is not clear, and, of course, that is the idea.

Around this time C. Aubrey Smith was organising matches for 'The Thespids', whenever he could get a team of actors together. Much later, in the early thirties, he provided a tremendous filip for the game in California with the Hollywood Cricket Club, and fellow actors Nigel Bruce, Boris Karloff, David Niven, H. B. Warner, and several others.

N. A. Knox, the Surrey and England fast bowler, understudied Basil Foster of Worcestershire in *The Dollar Princess* at Daly's Theatre.

The Rajah of Bhong appeared in *The Country Girl*, which had music by Lionel Monckton and lyrics from Adrian Ross, Percy Greenbank, and Paul Rubens. The Rajah, or rather Mr Rutland Barrington, sang a piece called PEACE, PEACE:

> *With a bat and a ball and a wicket,*
> *and we always have thought*
> *when we joined in the sport*
> *that we really were playing at cricket,*
> *but Australians came just to give us a game*
> *and although it is painful to say it*
> *they are teaching us fast, we are things of the past*
> *and we really don't know how to play it.*
> *Piece. Two innings apiece*
> *but nobody stayed very long*
> *Only Jessop and Mac could withstand the attack*
> *of our friends from the Valley of Bhong*
> *It's a blow to our pride that we can't find a side*
> *that can vanquish our cousins of Bhong.*

Mr Ronald Squire sang CRICKET IN NOVEMBER, for Messrs. George Grossmith and Edward Laurillard's Shaftesbury Theatre production of *Baby Bunting*, a musical play with lyrics by Clifford Grey and music by Nat D. Ayer.

Oscar Asche who told and produced that mystical tale of the east, 'Chu Chin Chow' played minor county cricket and sometimes Percy Fender who could score a century in a quicker time than it takes most of us to travel from the West End to the Oval appeared on stage.

The most controversial cricket tour ever made, that by Jardine's side to Australia in 1932/3, and the unleashing of Larwood, provoked an immediate response in the Theatre. Mr Cyril Ritchard who was appearing in *Our Miss Gibbs* at His Majesty's Theatre in Sydney, added an extra verse to his song.

> *Now this new kind of cricket takes courage to stick it*
> *There's bruises and fractures galore*
> *After kissing their wives and insuring their lives*
> *Batsmen fearfully walk out to score*
> *With a prayer and a curse, they prepare for the hearse*
> *Undertakers look on with broad grins*
> *Oh, they'd be a lot calmer in Ned Kelly's armour*
> *When Larwood the wrecker begins.*

At the Regent Theatre in Brisbane even REBECCA OF SUNNYBROOK FARM could not keep out of the act.

> *There's an Animal Test Match at Sunnybrook Farm*
> *And the Board of Control can't keep their calm*
> *For as soon as the centipede went into bat*
> *A cow bowled leg theory and knocked ten legs flat.*
>
> *Billy the Pig was next batsman in*
> *Then the cow bowled a fast one which cracked on his chin*
> *And a big lump of pig's cheek fell on the crease*
> *So they bound the cow over to keep the piece.*
>
> *Umpire Rebecca then took control*
> *And no balled the cow when he started to bowl*
> *So the ethics of cricket can suffer no harm*
> *If we follow Rebecca of Sunnybrook farm.*

Even today the tour has topicality. Christopher Douglas's radio play in 1980, *The Englishmen Abroad* re-enacts the whole grisly saga, though soon after the tour in 1933 London theatregoers had the chance to realise that cricket was after all only a game when they saw Ben Travers' Aldwych farce *A Bit of a Test*. Robertson Hare played the M.C.C. Captain touring Australia, and two more dissimilar characters than he and Jardine could not be imagined. At either end of the thirties there were plays with cricketing interest. The last Act of *Badgers Green* by R. C. Sherriff is set in the scorers' tent (the present author will hopefully be excused if he mentions that he played the third lead, Mr Twigg, with singular lack of distinction whilst at school), and J. B. Priestley's play *Johnson over Jordon* features an old cricket professional.

During the decade, the uncrowned king of English revue writers, Herbert Farjeon, introduced many a cricketing lyric into his work (some with music by Walter Leigh), and a recent production of *Farjeon Reviewed* at the Mermaid Theatre introduced a new musical setting by Ken Moule.

Reg Low wrote a concert party sketch *Cricket v Golf* for two characters — any male member of the Company and a comedian. It incorporated the names of members of the England team at the time, Leyland and Hammond, and in retrospect, seems very unfunny.

Eleanor Powell sang THAT'S NOT CRICKET, one hundred and ninety-eight times on Broadway in *At Home Abroad*, which was written by Howard Dietz and Arthur Schwartz. Others in the cast were Ethel Waters, Eddie Foy, Jnr., and Bea Lillie.

The Windmill Theatre, of fond memory for many, ran a 'Revuedeville', which was produced by Eve Bradfield. Rex Burrows, resident composer, and Paul Boyle of the *Daily Record* wrote a number called *Cricketing Girls of 1934*. It lent heavily on Gilbertian phrases like 'eleven maids in and eleven maids out', and inevitably had many a 'maiden over'.

The Stage C.C. was becoming established under the able and generous leadership of Garry Marsh, and its fixtures have shown the ability of many over the years — Russell Napier, Dennis Castle, William Franklyn, Abraham Sofaer, Oliver Battcock, Francis Mathews, and many more.

And during the period since the thirties, the allure of cricket has spread into so many dressing-rooms that it would seem now that a prerequisite for joining Equity is to be able to bat and bowl. The expansion of the media, one day games, sponsorship awareness have all helped.

The Theatre itself has seen plays with either passing or all-embracing cricket interest. Thomas Browne's *The Hat-Trick* had a heroine who was the Rachel Heyhoe-Flint of her day, Terence Rattigan's *The Winslow Boy*, Campbell Christie's *Come Live with Me*, Peter Watling's *Wilderness of Monkeys*, Alan Plater's *Simon Says*, Alan Ayckbourn's *Time and Time Again*, and then in 1979 Richard Harris's *Outside Edge*, which received the plaudits of critics and public alike, as every line caught an echo of their playing days.

The mixing of cricket with theatre is not a caucasian prerogative. In Barbados, the Bajan dialect drama *Bimshaw '73* has a character called Trevor Applethwaite, who scores a century against Lindwall, and the Asian immigration to Britain has given the chance for the Olympian Cricket Club to present Bachu Patel's musical bonanza *Sangeet Mela*.

Then, of course, since 1949, The Lord's Taverners, founded by a group of actors watching cricket from the Old Tavern at Lord's, have played many matches for charity, and their membership reads like a Who's Who of the entertainment business; there is now an Australian branch. THE TAVERNERS SONG, composed by Percy S. Robinson, who it will be remembered inscribed a song to Jack Hobbs in the 1930s, has been sung at many festive functions. The song which was dedicated by permission to Earl Alexander of Tunis when President of the M.C.C., is all about an old pewter tankard that was won by the author's great-grandfather on the village green when he was just twenty-one.

> *His score became history, at the local thatched inn*
> *They'd oft raise their tankards to William agin;*
> *And they'd speak of him proudly, his prowess and health*
> *And admire that old tankard that stands on the shelf.*

It was the Company of the Lord's Taverners that presented *Upgreen — and at 'em'*, or *'A Maiden Nearly Over'*, a cricketing melodrama with music in seven scenes and a denouement on BBC Television in June, 1960. Richard Attenborough was an umpire, Boris Karloff, a butler, Roger Livesey, a village squire, John Slater, a scoundrelly lawyer, Charlie Chester, a bookmaker, William Franklyn, a mysterious stranger, and Cardew Robinson was the Vicar. Tony Britton, Brian Reece, Garry Marsh, Ronald Shiner, Dudley Jones, Bruce Seton, Jack Warner, Sam Kydd, Jimmy Edwards, Peter Haigh, Brian Rix all represented the village or The Grange, and Martin Boddey, a founder member of The Taverners, was cast appropriately as the landlord of 'The Cricketers'. There were professional cricketers engaged as well, among them Doug Insole, Alf Gover, and Jack Martin, and just in case it was felt that there was a certain lack of refined vocal ability present, the George Mitchell Singers helped to dispel any doubts.

The Lord's Taverners had also helped present what was termed an Arenascope 'Bat and Ball' at the Radio Show, Earls Court six years earlier. The setting was for a single wicket match between five of Hambledon and five of All-England in the year 1781. Michael Denison, Tommy Trinder, Carleton Hobbs, MacDonald Hobley, Humphrey Lestocq all took part, and Norman Shelley played the Rev. Cotton, who by now needs no introduction. R. E. S. Wyatt, Tom Graveney, Keith Andrew, Alf Gover, and Alec Bedser made the All-England team; the umpires were Maurice Tate and George Duckworth, and the commentators Brian Johnston and John Arlott.

The mediums of television and radio have been the natural outlet for the imaginative cricket work whether it be purely historical, faction, fiction or fantasy. *Maiden Over*, an adaptation from Charles Hatton's novel *Sticky Wicket*, by C. Gordon Glover, *An Indispensable Rabbit* by Graham Clark, *The Cricket Match*, by Denis Constanduras, *The Fourth Stump*, and *Six Balls Out*, both by Blair, *The Atom Bowler*, by Jay and Stephen Black, *Jagger and the Magical Bat*, by Laurence Kitchen, *Panther Larkin*, by Simon Raven, and *One Eye Wild*, by Louis Macneice, which was a romance in commonplace, the portrait of a man who in poker terms would prefer his cards to be wild, who would like to be Homer, or Hector, or Hobbs, without having the hand for it. These, and recent offerings such as *Tales from the Long Room* by Peter Tinniswood, which takes an M.C.C. side to the Congo, have all married the worlds of cricket and drama. What could possibly be described as a marrying of music, cricket, and drama came with the broadcast in May of 1950, of a one-act operetta *The Batsman's Bride*, by Donald Hughes and Percy Heywood, though this had been first performed at Rydal School.

The variety shows have not lagged far behind. A Billy Cotton Band Show introduced THE CAPTAIN OF THE PRISON CRICKET TEAM, which had words by Bob Halfin and music by Harold Irving.

1 *That I was one of the M.C.C.*
  You never would have thought
  But as it happens the M.C.C's
  The Mar'lebone County Court.

  I bowled a copper out one day
  The judge said, 'You're a scream,
  We'll have to make you
  The captain of the Prison Cricket Team — So

  (chorus):
  I'm the captain of the prison cricket eleven,
  My number's ninety-seven
  Have breakfast at eleven-in-bed
  We will pinch the day for England
  Play up! Play up! The captain of the team.

> 2 *The Borstal Boys came for a match*
> *(They let them out on hire),*
> *Appearing sharp at half past two*
> *Inside a Black Maria.*
> *They hit the ball right over the wall*
> *It was a blinking shame,*
> *When Bill Sykes said 'I'll get it'*
> *And was never seen again. Oh!*

Don Spencer has introduced cricket into a recent effort WHAT'S A POMMIE that's sung by Rolf Harris.

'TV spells Magic' was a programme that included a couple of cricket numbers THE CRICKET GROUND QUARTET and CRICKET ON THE VILLAGE GREEN, the last title also being an item in a show in the West End, 'High Spirits'. Lance Percival sang CRICKET AND WIMBLEDON and CRICKET CALYPSO on Radio 4's 'Start the Week', and on the sound waves songs on cricket have been heard with increasing frequency [sic].

That group of high quality entertainers (how else can they be described?) 'Instant Sunshine', belied their name when singing ROLL ON THE COVERS to herald the start of the season on 'Stop the Week', another or Radio 4's intermittent perennials.

> *The season has started and cricket is here*
> *Unpack your bags and your cricketing gear*
> *Warm April days herald cricket again*
> *With spells of prolonged heavy rain.*
>
> *Roll on the covers lads, roll them on fast*
> *Cricket is here and it's summer at last*
> *Roll on the covers lads, rain has stopped play*
> *Drizzle's set in for the day.*

The group contributed an item on VILLAGE CRICKET for Thames Television's documentary on 'This Sporting Land'. They consist of three doctors and the former literary editor of *Punch*, and have been described by the *Sunday Times* as 'the thinking man's Rockers'. David Barlow, virtuoso performer on the 'spoons', is an excellent googly bowler, and once won a match for Trinity Triflers XI with an unbeaten innings of 11; Miles Kington, bassist, trombonist, jazz reviewer for *The Times,* captains a travelling *Punch* side; Alan Maryon-Davis, who plays exotic percussion and is the tragi-comic fall guy in the group has cricketing capabilities of an unknown quantity and quality, and finally and far from least, Peter Christie, who plays acoustic guitar, is lead singer, and writes all the material, and who played for Old Millhillians and the St George's Headstone Club in Harrow, describes himself as 'a mediocre all-rounder whose bowling has one purpose – to get as close to the wicket as possible!'

Another of their contributions to 'Stop the Week', was a few seasons ago when believe it or not there was a heatweave:

I was watching Middlesex and Hampshire play at Lord's
A fine game on a perfect Summer's day
The sun enhanced the view that Lord's Pavilion affords
And basking in the heat I studied play

Wearing my club blazer and my regimental tie
And straw hat which is now a little frayed
I watched a great tradition that will never fade or die
A game of county cricket being played

Little did I know that I was in for a surprise
A thunderbolt which shook me to the core
For there in the pavilion and before my very eyes
A man without a coat walked through the door

There he stood without a coat, no coat in Lord's Pavilion
He couldn't have been English, he was probably Brazilian
At least the bounder wore a tie, but one which hardly pleased the eye
A paisley pattern in a bright vermillion
The way the fellow sauntered by
Will haunt me till the day I die
There's nothing that can justify
No coat in Lord's Pavilion.

Leaping from my wicker chair I rushed to stop the cad
Who'd shamed the mecca of the MCC
But then I noticed dozens of the members had gone mad
For crowds of undressed men surrounded me
None of them were wearing coats, no coats in Lord's Pavilion
Were all these naked people ill or was it some rebellion
I'd never seen such goings on, with jackets and decorum gone
Quite suddenly the old place seemed quite alien
There was no blazer to be seen
The whole affair was quite obscene
I blush when I recall the scene
No coat in Lord's Pavilion.

Cricket took a bitter blow upon that fateful day
And there in the pavilion strong men cried
Yet buttoning up their jackets some stood firm and did not sway
And showed there were still Englishmen with pride

If a fellow wore no coat, no coat in Lord's Pavilion
You knew he was a rascal or inveterate rapscallion
But since this frightful howd'yer do, I'm forced to take a different view
And radically alter my opinion
For glancing round that shirted crew
I noticed several friends I knew
And so I tookd my coat off too
No coat, no coat, no coat
In Lord's Pavilion.

Ah, how things have changed, as they did once before at Lord's within living memory. Consider how Mr Mildly Inhibited Briton had his eardrums rent asunder by the gleeful shouts, steel drums, and captivating calypsos of the West Indian contingent in 1950. Never again could he wander into his favourite ground clutching somewhat self-consciously two and a half rounds of cucumber and caerphilly, squat on the wooden benches, and by mid-afternoon sink into sequestered somnolence, knowing that his slumber would stay uninterrupted until he chose to awake.

The first West Indian victory over England in a Test Match in this country had their supporters invading the pitch in their hundreds.

Nowadays hordes of small boys make it a predictable ritual; then it was an infectuous, spontaneous, outburst of enthusiasm that delighted the whole crowd. A guitarist led the invading group in a calypso that celebrated their team's performance — the intrinsic rhythmic patterns weaving a spell that was broken finally by rapturous applause.

Calypsos defy straight musical notation, but the recording by Egbert Moore (Lord Beginner) and the Calypso Rhythm Kings, that was issued shortly afterwards, found a place that brings but one answer when asking for a song on cricket:

Cricket, lovely cricket,
At Lord's where I saw it;
Cricket, lovely cricket,
At Lord's where I saw it;
Yardley tried his best
But Goddard won the test,
They gave the crowd plenty fun;
Second Test and West Indies won.

Chorus:
With those two little pals of mine
Ramadhin and Valentine.

The King was there well attired,
So they started with Rae and Stollmeyer;
Stolly was hitting balls around the boundary,
But Wardle stopped him at twenty.
Rae had confidence,
So he put up a strong defence;
He saw the King was waiting to see,
So he gave him a century.

Chorus:
With those two little pals of mine
Ramadhin and Valentine.

West Indies first innings total was
three-twenty-six
Just as usual.
When Bedser bowled Christiani
The whole thing collapsed quite easily,
England then went on,
And made one-hundred-fifty-one;
West Indies then had two-twenty lead,
And Goddard said, 'That's nice indeed'.

Chorus:
With those two little pals of mine
Ramadhin and Valentine.

Yardley wasn't broken-hearted
When the second innings started,
Jenkins was like a target
Getting the first five into his basket.
But Gomez broke him down,
While Walcott licked them around;
He was not out for one-hundred and sixty-eight,
Leaving Yardley to contemplate.

Chorus:
The bowling was super-fine,
With those two little pals of mine
Ramadhin and Valentine.

West Indies were feeling homely,
Their audience had them happy.
When Washbrook's century had ended,
West Indies' voices all blended.
Hats went in the air.
They jumped and shouted without fear;
So at Lord's was the scenery
Bound to go down in history.
Chorus:
After all was said and done,
Second Test and West Indies won!

A follow-up calypso from Lord Beginner was released after the First Test at Sabina Park, Kingston, Jamaica, in 1954, when the West Indies beat England by 140 runs. This calypso has a slower, more hypnotic beat, and the undertones beneath the triumphant notes jar slightly, and hint at the uneasy atmosphere in which the match was played,

West Indies and England met once again,
Stollmeyer beat Hutton with feather brain

and then the Chorus: *They can't beat the West Indies at all*, or is that reading too much into a situation which had Jeffrey Stollmeyer booed for not enforcing the follow-on, and physical attacks on the family of one of the umpires? Calypsos, after all, do tend to reflect the consensus thought of those watching the events they describe.

Rancour caused by umpiring decisions was the theme of another calypso, this time from Lord Kitchener, accompanied by Coleman's Calypso Boys.

The M.C.C. proclaim that they are not pleased
about some unfair decision in the West Indies

This time, however, the mood is conciliatory and the calypso, which has a languid 'feel', is full of charm,

Oh, we ask you please, do not blame the
West Indies.

Lord Kitchener, or Aldwyn Roberts to give him his proper name, produced a calypso called THE CRICKET SONG in 1964, which drew on highlights of the West Indian tour of England in the year before:

> *England was in trouble from the very start*
> *Hall and mighty Griffith really broke their heart*
> *At a hundred miles per hour*
> *They made the ball fly*
> *The Englishmen bawl, 'Umpire,*
> *We appeal for light.'*

(chorus):
> *Hall, Griffith*
> *Don't stop at all*
> *Hall, Griffith*
> *Give em' back the ball*
> *Hall, Griffith,*
> *Sobers and Hall*
> *Hall, Griffith*
> *Bring Gibbs an' all*

And so it continues, extolling the virtues of wicket-keeper Murray and others in the side. More recent calypsos have been CRICKET '76 by R. Coke and sung by Tony Dee, and WHO'S GROVELLING NOW by E. Gray, and sung by Ezeike, which was a reaction to an unfortunate remark by Tony Greig that received much publicity. A CRICKET CALYPSO that equals the best of its kind in humour and originality, and delighted the 1980 West Indian side to Great Britain, was by David Henry Wilson,

> *De West Indians have come to town*
> *To hit de ball all over de groun'.*
> *De English dey struggle wid might an' main . . .*
> *To get de Lord to send down de rain.*

> *Clive Lloyd de captain takes all de pressure,*
> *Lookin' like an absent-minded professor.*
> *De way to dismiss a man of his class is*
> *To get short leg to breathe on his glasses.*

De vice-captain's Somerset's Richards Viv,
De greatest Antiguan dat ever did live.
To catch him you've got one chance in a million —
Put all your fielders inside de pavilion.

Gordon Greenidge is only in clover
If he can reach 50 in de first over.
Des Haynes smiles bright as de sun in de sky,
But if you run him out he'll have a good cry.

De English complain dat Kallicharan
Don't look like a proper West Indi-an.
An' lightin' Bacchus is anudder man
Dey wish was playin' for Pakistan.

Collis King hits as hard as a ragin' lion,
An' de fielders could do wid gloves of iron.
Derek Parry takes wickets, as much as you need,
But can't play in Tests 'cos he's de wrong speed.

De wicket-keeper's a source of worry —
Should it be D. Murray, or should it be D. Murray?
Poor Lawrence Rowe's suffered more dan a little —
Two hours in de field means two weeks in hospital.

De fast bowlers' union is very strong,
When dey strike negotiations don't last long.
De sight of Croft causes many alarms,
He bowls like a windmill wid six arms.

Malcolm Marshall runs like Olympic sprinter,
An' de batsman's bat turns into a splinter.
An' Holding runs from so far in de deep,
By de time he arrives de batsman's asleep.

Roberts frowns like he's feelin' too sick to play,
But de batsman's de one dat limps away.
De English say Big Joel's bowlin' ain't cricket —
He leans down de pitch an' drops de ball straight on de wicket.

> *De West Indians have come to town*
> *To hit de ball all over de groun'.*
> *I wish de whole worl' learnt to play*
> *Cricket de Caribbean way.*

There's even a Trueman Calypso — one that was sung by singer Ronnie Hilton at a Variety Show in Blackpool, although it is arguable if there is any such thing as an English calypso. Calypsos need that freedom of expression and lack of inhibition which is intrinsic to the black soul, and makes it such an exiting ethnic musical form. The best calypsos rely on sheer improvisation, and as such their nearest neighbour is some forms of jazz.

Fred Trueman had a cabaret club act, and issued a single RED IS RED AND BLUE IS BLUE, and there is no doubt that fast bowlers lend themselves to song. WE GOT THOMMO reminded Australians that Jeff Thomson was a potent striking force. The record was not released in England — perhaps that was kindness on the part of the distributors.

A song that was from a different kettle altogether came from the extremely talented Richard Stilgoe. The song LILIAN THOMSON is one of over a dozen cricket songs that are the product of an agile and highly inventive mind. Stilgoe's speed in composition is staggering — which is what a lot of English supporters felt that they were about to do when hearing the news of the sad collapse of their side's batting against that terrifying lady,

> *Ev'ry morning on the radio, the news comes to Australia*
> *The English batsmen once again have had a ghastly failure*
> *It was Lilian Thomson's bowling once again caused the collapse*
> *I always thought Test Cricket was intended just for chaps*
> *But Lilian Thomson is Australia's finest flower*
> *A maiden bowling overs at a hundred miles an hour.*

She's the fastest lady bowler that the world has ever seen
Her bumper's awe-inspiring and her language far from clean
Just imagine the reaction of Greig or Knott or Amiss
As this six foot six of Sheila runs up, do you wonder they miss?

She hit Randall on the ankle, then she hit him on the forehead
She finds the happy medium she could hurt him something horrid.

She's Lilian Thomson, the first of cricket's dames
A mixture of Joan Sutherland, Rolf Harris, or Clive James
She'll hit you on the temple, in the groin or knee and kidney,
To prove that liberated Adelaide's as good as Sydney.

Richard Stilgoe wrote, sang, and accompanied himself on the piano in a number of skilfully woven cricket songs for BBC Radio 4's Serendipity programmes on 'The Patrons of Cricket', and 'The First Test'. 'The Patrons of Cricket' was presented by that distinguished 'Sort of Cricket Person' E. W. Swanton, and Stilgoe risked what might best be described as papal wrath by starting one song on a certain Australian entrepeneur with sentiments akin to 'Why on earth do they all get at poor old Kerry Packer?' An exercise in support of democratic thought was never needed, however, with a person of 'Jim' Swanton's stature and humour.

The First Test was adeptly presented by Tim Rice, and contained 'live' commentary from the scene of the 1877 match by Brian Johnston. There were three songs, the last of which could be called *Two Hundred Years of Cricket*.

In Melbourne on the Ides of March in 1877
The English team encountered an Australian eleven,
They couldn't see how possibly an English team could fail,
Although that chap behind the stumps could not get out on bail,
'We'll show the convicts how,' they cried,
'We'll play these chaps alive.'
But as you know it wasn't so
They lost by forty-five.

In nineteen seventy seven to proclaim the century,
Another team of Englishmen went to the colony,
'Your Chappell's and your Lillee's don't scare me,' cried Tony Greig,
And Lillee chewed his gum, and bowled, and hit him on the leg.
And Randall scored a century, but still t'was all in vain
T'was just the same, we lost the game by forty-five again.

In twenty seventy seven, when the bi-centenary's played
What bumpers will be bowled, how many centuries made?
As in the Cornhill, Texaco, John Player, Dunhill Test,
The Aussies in their Brearley patent caps take on the rest
As Arlott, Johnson, Frindall in the commentary box in heaven
Compare them to the English team of nineteen seventy seven
One thing is sure, the final score, however hard they strive
Our national pride, the England side will lose by Forty-five!

Richard Stilgoe also has found inspiration from an English fast bowler abroad, SNOW IN THE WEST INDIES.

The obscenities in rugger songs have never quite been matched by those on cricket, though the latter lack nothing in *doubles entendres*.

Sticky Wicket Blues

I got the blues — my baby's bereft me
I said the blues — my baby's done left me
To put it bluntly I've been knackered
Damn well Kerry Packered
Got that damn shame it ain't cricket Blues.

I got the Blues — I dropped it at mid-on
I said the Blues — couldn't keep the lid on
My delivery is dickey
My wicket's feeling sticky
Got that damn shame it ain't cricket Blues.

My baby was a yorker corker
Played her ball and bat
Kissed her near the pavilion — shouted 'Howzat!'
Thought she might go the whole hog
Tried to keep my grip
The only thing I kept up — was my stiff upper lip.

My baby she said, 'Buck up!
Let's get laid!'
Began some slap and tickle — I said, 'Old girl — well played!'
I said, 'Play the game at home'
She said, 'No, have it away'
We got a little near the knuckle — then thank God bad light stopped play.

The work of actor/singer Jonathan Adams; I suppose it could be said to be complemented by an adaptation of Pete Seeger's version of LITTLE BOXES by West Country singer Fred Wedlock who alone seems to have had the courage to contravene the rather genteel code by which commentators and writers will perform extraordinary euphemistic contortions, in order to avoid using the word 'testicles',

BOXES

Little boxes in the sports shop
Little boxes are for cricketers
Little boxes made of plastic
Little boxes, all the same.
There's a white one and a pink one
And one made of aluminium
For the tender bits of cricketers
And it still hurts quite a lot.

And the batsmen still get injured
And get impotent and quite undignified
'Cos a short ball in the boxes
Hurts the ballses quite a lot;
There's a green one and a pink one
And a blue one and a yellow one
With a sprinkling of aluminium
And it still hurts quite a lot.

As has been said, the Dorset group 'The Yetties', who have a deservedly popular following far beyond their own county, have added musical accompaniment to the lyrics of John Arlott in a sequence of annual BBC Radio 3 programmes 'The Sound of Cricket', 'The Echoing Green', 'The Sound of Bat and Ball', and 'Sounds of Summer'. The idea for 'The High Catch' came from the occasion when Bonnor skied Alfred Shaw at the Oval in 1880, and he and his partner had run two before Fred Grace caught him at point.

THE HIGH CATCH

1 *The stranger hit that mighty skier*
  For height there was no matching it
  Up it went and higher and higher
  Who was the man for catching it?

2 *The captain watched it climbing high*
  And wondered who to send for it
  The bowler cocked a baleful eye
  At those at the other end for it.

3 *No one wanted that risky prize*
  To call on long stop would be wrong
  Once he sighted it in his eyes
  Our long stop he did not stop long.

4 *We thought the wicket keeper should*
  He had the gloves, but made a fuss
  'Twas not his job he said but would
  Lend his gloves to one of us.

5 *Meanwhile the batsmen ran and ran*
  Two dozen had gone on the board
  The captain found no catching man
  And still that red ball soared and soared.

6 *Where was the man who struck the blow?*
  His bat lay there scorched by flame
  No one knew him nor saw him go
  The score book did not name his name.

7 *No one wanted that awful catch*
  Climbing from that stranger's stroke
  Who in a moment won the match
  And vanished in a puff of smoke.

8 *If climbed and climbed right out of sight*
  Never even began to fall
  They waited all that day and night
  But devil a sight saw of that ball.

9 *The umpire he feared to shout 'lost ball'*
  But when his final judgement came
  He gave as his impartial call
  'This cricket is a hell of a game'.

(chorus):
Too high in the sky
Oh, not I not I.

An anonymous bowler philosophises on his bowling technique, or maybe he just 'tickles it with his spinnin' finger'

1 *A tickle o' me spinnin' finger*
  The finest bowler in our village I be
  Though there's some says I'm a slinger
  But I bowls with me brains and acc'racy
  And a tickle of me spinnin' finger
  A tickle of me spinnin' finger

2 *I gets 'em out, though I ain't very bright*
  Nor fast nor much of a swinger
  With a steady length, a little bit of flight
  And a tickle of me spinnin' finger
  A tickle of me spinnin' finger

3 *I gets all peevish when me faster ball*
  Gets edged and it flies a stinger
  To second slip and he lets it fall
  Through the tickle of me spinnin' finger
  A tickle of me spinnin' finger

4 *I loves catchin' batsmen on the hop*
  With the quick bounce of me springer
  Which leaps with just a little bit o' top
  And a tickle of me spinnin' finger
  A tickle of me spinnin' finger

5 *I loves our umpire's daughter Ann,*
  And if she'll marry me I'll bring her
  All of the money and the love I can
  And a tickle of me spinnin' finger
  A tickle of me spinnin' finger.

The Yetties, who are Pete Shutler, the musician of the group, Mac McCulloch 'the handsome one', Bob Common, who has now left, known as 'the amicable water-butt', and the studious scribe, Bonny Sartin, who has a couple of cricket songs of his own to his credit. CRICKET ON THE

VILLAGE GREEN is one, and the other was requested by the Somerset County Cricket Club:

>1 *Get yer coat, get yer hat*
> *Polish up yer old howzat*
> *Come and cheer for the team*
> *That plays like a dream*
> *Somerset, Somerset*
> *The best in all the land that's Somerset.*

2 *Brian leads, Vic Succeeds*
 Roebuck's a man of deeds
 Viv is great, Kitch first rate
 And Currie bowls em straight
 Somerset, Somerset
 The best in all the land that's Somerset
 Some Some Some Somerset, Somerset
 Some some summer we'll beat all comers
 Some Some Somerset.

3 *Jennings spins, Ian wins*
 And Gardie keeps the pins
 Dennis jokes, Dasher strokes
 To catche em we've got Slokes
 Somerset, Somerset
 The best in all the land that's Somerset

4 *Hallam Strives, Burgess drives*
 Derrick loves the dives
 Dredgie swings, Olive stings
 And Big Bird's got his wings
 Somerset, Somerset
 The best in all the land that's Somerset
 Som, Som, Somerset, Somerset
 Some, some summer we'll beat all comers
 Som, Som, Somerset.

5 *So get yer bat, get yer hat*
 Polish up yer old howzat
 Come and cheer for the team
 That are picked from the cream
 Somerset, Somerset,
 The best in all the land that's Somerset.

Perceval Graves was the son of A. P. Graves of *Zummerzet varsus Zurrey*, and half-brother to Robert Graves, the poet. In the last years of his life he was living in King's Langley, Hertfordshire, though in his booklet *More Songs and Snatches* he chose a different county — Lancashire,

Up North when we play the Yorkshire tykes
At the noble game of cricket,
Committee come in on their motor-bikes
To inspect Old Trafford wicket.
It's a stubborn struggle of brawn and brain,
Excitement will never diminish,
Though it's sure to end in a draw or rain,
At Leeds, we play it all over again:
Ay, Manchester's right, it's not polite
To fight it out to a finish.

There are two more items on cricket in the booklet *When the Meadows are aglow*, and *Phyllis at the wicket*. Naturally Cupid's not far from the end of her bat, and she easily secures a very willing victim.

The Lancashire County Cricket Club gave permission for the dedication to them of SUNSHINE, which has words and music by Leslie Haworth. The song has been recorded by The Spinners, one of the country's finest folk groups. It is all about a Lancashire fan taking the day off work to go and watch the Roses match. It takes a lot to stop him going: *If Gulbenkian should offer me one thousand pounds, to stay away from the cricket ground, I would reckon that money was really hard earned. Till he does I'm unconcerned.*

Cricket songs have arrived from many sides of the recording industry; there could not be two more dissimilar offerings than from The Singing Postman and The Kinks. The uncomplicated gentle strumming of the former is a world away from the sophisticated multi-tracked creations of a modern pop group. On their L.P. 'Preservation Act 1', which was issued in 1973 is CRICKET, THE VICAR — nothing I am sure to do with more formal connections between the canto and the crotchet. *Now God lay down the rules of life when he wrote those Ten Commandments, and to cricket those ten same rules shall apply.* The demon bowler is synonymous with the Devil, and *All thro' your life he'll try to bowl you out.*

In recent years there have been incursions into the cricketing arena that have been a sharp reminder of its fragile defence against the uncompromising and harrying world on its doorstep. Test match turf dug up by angry petitioners for George Davis, demonstrations against playing with Apartheid. Protest in violent form has become the norm, and yet sadly, sometimes cricket's only answer is in song.

GREEN GREEN FIELDS

This song, a parody on the Tom Jones' hit 'The Green Green Grass of Home', was written in protest at the decision to drive the extension of the 'Heads of the Valley' motorway through the Pontneathvaughan cricket ground. The 'Bont' as it is called, is reputed to be one of the oldest clubs in Wales.

It was a great shame, therefore, to see that road driven unnecessarily through such a lovely, picturesque little ground. The club true to its great tradition still flourishes, but sadly cricket is no longer played in the village of 'Pontneddfechan'.

Now it's never been the same
Since that news from London came,
Games are cancelled now but not for any rain.
Down Bont Road I look with tears-a-falling,
'Cos I can see bulldozers crawling,
Why can't they leave our Green Green Field alone?
But they'll bring that ugly concrete highway,
To take away what once was my way,
Why can't they leave our Green Green Field alone?

The old Club House is still standing,
Though the paint is cracked and dry,
And there's that one-armed bandit that we used to play on.
Down that road I look with tears a-falling,
'Cos I can see a Euclid crawling.
Why can't they leave our Green Green Field alone?

But as I bat and look around me,
I realize that surveyor wasn't joking.
'Cos they'll bring that ugly concrete highway
And take away what once was my way.
Why can't they leave our Green Green Field alone?
Yes, they'll bring that ugly concrete highway
And take away what once was my way,
Why can't they leave our Green Green Field alone?

They have thundered through the hills,
Past the streams and watermills.
They have turned our little valley floor to stone.
They have broken through the farms and churches,
Lovely oaks and silver birches.
Why can't they leave our Green Green Field alone?
But we'll fight although we ain't got money,
(I've got a Butty in the Free Wales Army!)
Why can't they leave our Green Green Field alone.

A song from that effervescent Welshman, Max Boyce. Another in similar vein has been written by Bruce Ogston, who was a chorister at Salisbury Cathedral, and later won the Elizabeth Schumann Prize for Lieder singing, and a Leverhulme Scholarship.

AND DID THOSE FEET

Listen well to our song, it's not a time for mirth;
For all you know it won't be long, before they spoil your turf.
When politicians loudly claim that we're a violent nation,
They darn well ought to lay the blame on lack of recreation.
When next we sing 'and did those feet', remember who marched over
The pitch where once we used to meet in white pads and pullover.
And now that we're without a ground, with nowhere to play ball,
Come next weekend we'll all be found sat in the Bingo Hall.

They're digging up our pitch to lay a pipeline
Our well-trod green will soon become a ditch;
It seems a crying shame to take away our game,
Just to make some blinkin' business magnate rich.
We reckon that they've got a bloody nerve
In offering us a ground ten miles away;
We politely said 'no thanks' — we're not prepared to fill our tanks
And drive the twenty miles each cricket day.

*No more the fading Summer sun will give us time to score
A badly needed final run, no more the stumps we'll draw.
Bats, caps and pads we'll put in store, and if it is too long
Before we win the toss once more, we'll all be dead and gone.
Our pitch so green and full of peace, our men all clad in white,
The scoreboard and the waiting crease, all vanished overnight.
And where last year, our rival town once met their Waterloo,
They've set an ugly cabin down that's called a Portaloo.*

*They're plundering our pitch to lay a pipeline,
They estimate about a year or two:
But with the mess they've made, it'll be a good decade —
In the meantime what are we supposed to do?
We're told that Britain badly needs more fuel
And they've gone and struck oil somewhere very near,
So our pitch must take a beating for the sake of central heating
Grace would say it's a disgrace if he were here.*

*They've robbed us of our pitch to lay a pipeline
It's enough to cause our British blood to boil.
We fail to understand why they can't use other land
And pipe their oil through someone else's soil.
We've petitioned our MP and all Westminster
We've even marched with banners down the street,
But if our petition fails, we'll never burn our bails
Or let them think that we accept defeat.*

*So watch out all you chaps who love your cricket
If it looks as if they're threatening your wicket,
Stand up for the Nation, accept no compensation
Just speak up strong and tell them where to stick it
Stick it, stick it, stick it — their putrid pipeline —
Just speak up strong and tell them where to stick it!*

Songs about and by touring parties have always been part of any cricketing trip. Some become a sort of happy *leitmotif* for a close-knit group, and are forgotten as soon as the tour is over; others filter through to feed some commercial interests, and then are soon lost in public indifference. A few last longer, by chance or intrinsic worth and one such is A SONG OF THE FAST BOWLER which remains from Fitzgerald's trip to North America in 1872. Major Warton's team to South Africa, which frequently tottered onto the field through incessant hospitality, sang themselves hoarse at nightly entertainments when made-up ditties, ballads, and songs from the Kaffir were often led by the robust baritone of C. Aubrey Smith; none of these have stood time's test.

Ray Illingworth's victorious M.C.C. team sang THE ASHES SONG — 70/71. Vic Lewis, who runs his own cricket XI, and has done much for charitable causes, was the musical director, and the arrangement was by Ken Thorne:

We've got the Ashes back home
We've got them in the urn
The Aussies have had them twelve years
So we've got to have our turn.

The reverse side of the record was a version of HULLO DOLLY that had a new ending, *The Ashes won't ever go away again.* They were lost three years later!

Mind you, that was a little after the Australian side of 1972 had predicted:

Here come the Aussies
and cricket is the game
We're all together
and winning is our aim.
So, we'll play on thro' the English rain
And win the Ashes back again.

The English weather seemed to be a fixation with the team, as on the other side of the disc was heard BOWL A BALL, SWING A BAT

Ev'ry time we play our game
Hold a catch, win the match
Even thro' the rain.

Touring teams tend to follow the coach party tradition of introducing as many *appropriate* variations as possible to well-known tunes. Even hymns are not exempt. In living memory an M.C.C. side touring India changed WHAT A FRIEND WE HAVE IN JESUS to WHEN THIS BLOODY TOUR IS OVER, NO MORE INDIA FOR ME. It will always be the same.

Kerry Packer's circus — World Series Cricket, which has helped change the face of the game in the last few years, sponsored musical jingles that enveloped the air waves seemingly at the end of every over. And then there was the song. To be in Australia in 1978 was to be haunted by C'MON AUSSIE, C'MON C'MON. If familiarity really does breed contempt, then constant repetition becomes a drug from which it is very difficult to obtain release

> *Lillee pounds them down like a machine*
> *Pascoe's making divets in the green*
> *Marsh is taking wickets*
> *Hookes'ys clearing pickets*
> *And the Chappell's eyes are back to the green.*

Cricket's music, and the sometimes looser connection between performers in both fields will undoubtedly continue. We have but touched on the unbroken line since pre-Hambledonian days, and if the concentration has been on the product rather than the practitioner, then that is not to demean the musical talents of many an able cricketer.

There were the Lyttleton brothers, Edward and Spencer, who together formed the bass line for the Free Forester part song quartette, and there are many other names which jostle for space. Surrey's O'Gorman brothers, who made many a Music Hall echo with trombone, the Essex all-rounder James Cutmore who awoke those same echoes with his voice, the violin of Kent's Colin Blythe, and the tenor saxophone of Surrey and England fast bowler Maurice Allom. Allom, incidentally, was a member of a Cambridge University group called the Quinquaginta Club Ramblers, who were led by the well-known jazz pianist Fred Elizalde. The group was good enough to attract a recording contract, and several titles were issued by Brunswick.

Another player who performed in a traditional jazz group was trombonist Frank Parr, a Lancashire wicket keeper of the fifties.

More recently, Cambridge contemporaries Eddie Craig, Lancashire opening bat, and two England captains, Tony Lewis of Glamorgan and

Mike Brearley of Middlesex, have continued the musical tradition. Craig as a pianist, Brearley on clarinet, and Lewis as leader of the National Youth Orchestra of Wales.

As for musicians of more or less renown who have played cricket, the list is endless, so let us make an imperfect cadence with the Rossall School XI and Thomas Beecham.

When covering cricket's fraternity with the world of entertainment there was deliberate avoidance of the game on film. Well over thirty feature films have included cricket as part of the setting, some with the game integral to the story, others using it as dressing, but consideration of the output which has encompassed the traditional scenario of THE FINAL TEST, and the futuristic experiments of space odyssey THE BIG HIT, will have to be left to another book. Suffice to say that music composed for cricketing moments on these films can logically qualify as cricket music. As a throwaway to the subject here, it is worth remembering that the Pakistani batsman Haroon Rashid's father is a celebrated film director in his own country, and that the international film star Omar Sharif, who has received a lot of publicity for his skill at poker, received far less as an unknown cricketer captaining an Egyptian touring side to England.

Leaving the best till last is a technique that seldom palls, even when risking a qualitative statement over something as emotive as a song, which is usually a foolhardy exercise. And yet with Roy Harper's WHEN AN OLD CRICKETER LEAVES THE CREASE released in 1975, and dedicated to John Snow and Geoff Boycott, the temptation is strong. A simple uncluttered guitar accompaniment later supported by brass band that gives a suitable earthy 'feel', a haunting melody that improves with each re-hearing, and a nostalgic poignant lyric, all help make a superbly realised work of art. Obviously the overall effect cannot be gleaned from the words alone, though they hint at the imaginative potential. Testimony to the song's calibre has come from disc jockey Tony Blackburn, who described it as the pop song of the seventies. It is more than that — far more. It is in essence *the* cricket song.

When the day is done
and the ball has spun
in the umpire's pocket away
and all remains in the groundman's pains
for the rest of time and a day.
There'll be one mad dog and his master
Pushing for four with the spin
On a dusty pitch
with two pound six
of willow wood in the sun.

When an old cricketer leaves the crease
You never know whether he's gone
If sometimes you're catching a fleeting glimpse
of a twelfth man at silly mid-on.
And it could be Geoff and it could be John
with the new ball sting in his tail
And it could be me and it could be thee
And it could be the sting in the ale.

When the moment comes in the gathering stands
And the clock turns back to reflect
on the years of grace as those footsteps trace
For the last time out of the act
Well this way of life's recollection
The hallowed strip in the haze
the fabled men and the noonday sun
are much more than just yarns of their days.

When an old cricketer, etc.

(Words and music Roy Harper
©Great Western Myths Ltd./Blackhill Music Ltd.
Recorded on Roy Harper album 'HQ', EMI SHVL)

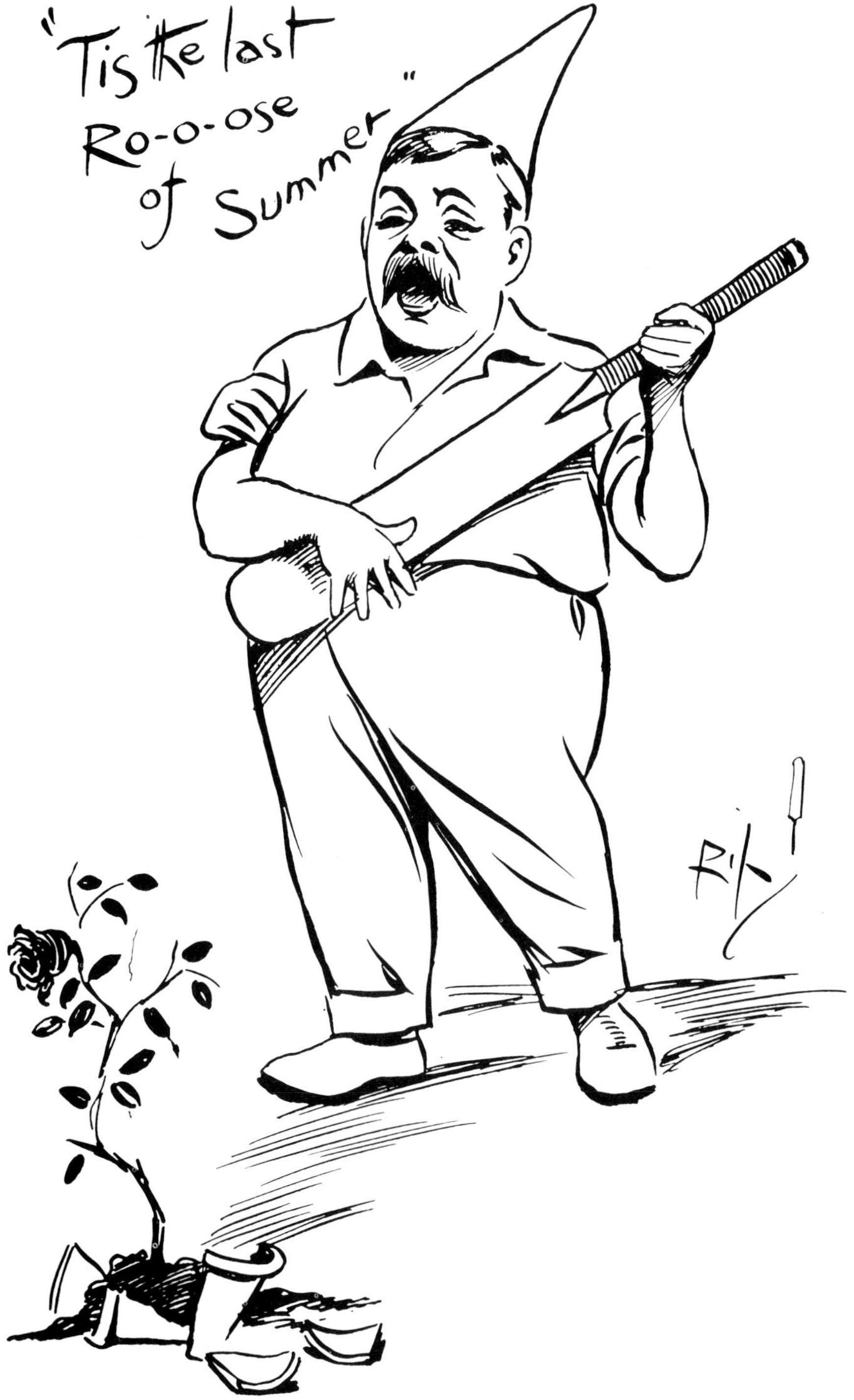
"Tis the last
Ro-o-ose
of Summer"
Rix

APPENDIX

The following list could be described as a combination of cricket songography and musicography though both terms are unwieldy and ugly labels for what is no more than a catalogue of cricket music that has been noted when preparing this volume. It cannot hope to be comprehensive, some of the items only contain a passing reference, and it is quite likely that a few titles under *Cricket* refer to the insect and not the game, culled as they were from card indices at the Performing Rights Society. It is easy to be misled, certainly *Cricket* by the fifteenth century contrapuntist Josquin des Près has nothing to do with bat and ball, and perhaps less surprisingly nor has a modern number called *Confessions of a Bouncer*.

As far as I know, there is no really substantial list of cricketing music existing in the public domain at the time of writing, and therefore it is hoped that the catalogue, though lacking detailed information for many of the entries, will help fill the gap.

Advice Gratis (dedicated to F. Stanley Jackson)	*Gale, Wynne Wright & Co. c. 1890*
Agar the Dutchman (contains phrase 'bowl for it, bat for it')	
Aislabie's Cricketing Alphabets	
The Alert Club	
The All England Eleven and the Ashun Chaps	*Samuel Laycock*
All Hail to Cricket (Air – 'John Barleycorn')	
And did those feet	*Bruce Ogston, 1980*
The annual Cricket Match: a musical quiz	*Frank Butterworth, 1965*
Archibald certainly not	
Around the field at Haverford	*Ralph D. Paine*
The Ashes Song, 70/71	*Johnston, Lewis, Henderson*
Assist all ye Muses (two different versions)	*adpt. Rev. R. Cotton (18th c.)*
The Asylum Cricket Match	*Edward Kent, Reynolds & Co.*
A Tickle o' me spinnin' finger	*Arlott, The Yetties, 1977*
Australian Cricketers Chorus (Pot Pourri, an 1899 Review)	*W. H. Risque, Napoleon Lambelet, Boosey & Co.*
The Australian Eleven Galop	*C.E. Pratt, W.H. Glen & Co*

The Ballade of the Slogger	*Joseph Baron*
The Batsman's Bride: an operetta	*Donald Hughes, Percy M. Heywood O.U.P. Copyright, 1957*
A Batsman's Song	*Greville E. Matheson, Francis Thorns, 1914, Weekes & Co.*
The Battle of the Blues	*Abel Kidd, 'Old Stump', 1873*
The Big Match of 1892 (tune Killaloo) (Matches between Royal and St. Thomas)	*Ceylon*
Billy Brown of Bradford Town	
The Birth of the Ashby-de-la-Zouch C.C	*1826*
' Bob ' Abel (Tune — Annie Rooney)	*A. Craig*
Bowl a ball, Swing a bat	*Daniel Boone, Rod McQueen, 1972*
The Boy's Cricket Song — sung by Mr Sam Dalton (Tune — I want a girl)	
The Boys of Merry England: Quadrilles	*C. H. R. Marriott*
Bradman 238	*S.E.N.*
Brown of Brighton	*Arlott, 1977, The Yetties*
Brunswick Cricket Song	
Bushwacker Ballads	
The Captain of a Prison Cricket Team	*Bob Halfin, Harold Irving*
Carmen Aestivum (Tonbridge School)	*G. L. Herman, Thomas Wood, 1920*
Carmen Marburiense	
A Chant for the Yorkshire Champion	*Lewis Hall, 1883*
The Chief of British Pastimes: song respectfully dedicated to the Cricketers of England. Written and composed by John Hutson (patronized by H.R.H. The Prince of Wales)	*Symphony and accompaniment by George Roe, Chappell & Co.*
The City Charltonian Cricket Club incl. To the Field; Cricket is a Noble Game; The Eleven; Come boys come; Love the merry, merry pastime; The Lover of Cricket	*C. Jolly, 1857*

Clark's Sporting Songs	
C'mon Aussie c'mon (Mojo Singers)	*Allan Johnston & Alan Morris, W.E.A.*
The Colony (Borth Song — Uppingham)	*E. Thring, P. David, 1876*
Come all good people (Tune — Lucy Long)	*Sung by Mr Hartopp*
Come to the Gabba	*Wilkes, Postlewaithe Wayne Roberts, R.C.A. 1975*
Concerning Cricket	*L.G.T.*
Cricket	*Raymond Davies*
Cricket	*G. Franks, E. Merriman*
Cricket	*Maynard J. Grover, Derek McCulloch, 1933*
Cricket	*V. de Leath, Ray Henderson, Louis Bureau*
Cricket	*Heault, Thompson*
Cricket	*Koenig*
Cricket	*Mike McNaught, Ken Martine*
Cricket	*H. G. L. Mills, Edmund Forman, 1889*
Cricket	*Morley*
Cricket	*Henry Newbolt*
Cricket	*Terry Short*
Cricket	*Mike Simpson*
Cricket	*Tackett*
Cricket: comic song	*Dick Henry, 1935*
Cricket (Country House Ditties) (dedicated to I. Zingari)	*H. & L Trevor and A Scott-Batty Boosey, 1898*
Cricket (Dance band no.)	*Edward White*
Cricket (dedicated to cricketing carthusians)	*B. C. Stephenson, Lionel Monckton*
Cricket, 1877 (Upside Down)	*Richard Stilgoe*

Cricket (March)	Max Geiger, 1939
Cricket (No. 2 Happy School Days)	Heller, Nicholls
Cricket (pfte.)	Barbara Moore, 1974
Cricket (pfte.)	J. Warner, 1939
Cricket (polka)	Warren-Phillips, Gregory
Cricket: a song	W. G. Hartnell, V. Wilson. Song Success Syndicate, 1923
Cricket: a song	G. A. Hicks, 1900. John Farmer, J. Williams
Cricket (S. F. Lank Sal U Lewe)	Sam Sklair
Cricket (Ten Songs for Children)	Rummel, 1914
Cricket (Unison Song)	Joseph Bealieu – Lengnick
Cricket – The Vicar (Preservation Act 1)	The Kinks
Cricket (vocal)	Charles Wolsely, 1937. Newman
Cricket After Grace	Felix Dumas and Harry Adams. F.D.H.
(The) Cricket and the Bat (A Natural History Match in Three Innings and a Musical Score)	Harry Gifford and Alf J. Lawrance, 1914, F.D.H.
Cricket and Wimbledon	Lance Percival
Cricket and the Witchdoctor (Musical Monologue)	Kenneth Western, 1958
Cricket at Worcester (voice and pfte.)	John Gould, Frederick Grice, 1971
(The) Cricket Ball Sings	E. V. Lucas
Cricket Bat Boogie (The Shadows)	Marvin, Welch, ATV Music
(The) Cricket Bat – an emblem of peace (A digest of cricketing facts and fears 'A Spectator' Esq.)	'Bat', F. Platts, 1863
(The) Cricket Bat Polka (dedicated to W. G. Grace)	Henry A. Sutch, Charles Sheard
Cricket Batting / Cricket Bowling Sports Coaching Series	Sam Sklair
Cricket Calypso	Peter Akister, MS
Cricket Calypso (voice and pfte.)	Bill McGuffie, Colin Bostock Smith

Cricket Calypso	*Lance Percival*
Cricket Calypso	*David Henry Wilson, 1980*
Cricket Carols	*Kenneth Rankin*
Cricket Champions (Kitch '67)	*Aldwyn Roberts*
(The) Cricket Champions (West Indies v England 1954)	*Lord Beginner and Caribbean Calypso Band*
(The) Cricket Champions, 1954 (Lord Beginner)	*Egbert Moore*
Cricket for Clerics	*Brett Stevens, Alan Reeve-Jones*
(The) Cricket Club, blackballing a member	*1869*
Cricket Commentary	*Edwin Joseph Ayong, Gary Dore*
Cricket Cradle Songs	*L.*
Cricket Crazy	*Con Rosselson*
Cricket, Cricket	*Bill Oddie*
Cricket excitement (Calypso)	*Terry Nelson, 1972. Guyana*
Cricket Fever	*Kenneth Western, 1956*
(The) Cricket Game (Calypso)	*Frank Atwell, 1956. Cucumber Music*
Cricket Ground Quartet (TV Spells Magic)	*Cass, Myers*
Cricket I Sing	*Stephen Phillips, 1913*
Cricket in Eden (opener)	*Richard Stilgoe*
Cricket in November (Baby Bunting)	*Nat D. Ayer, Clifford Grey, 1919, Feldman & Co.*
Cricket in Time Square (Incidental Music)	*M. J. S. Clarke*
Cricket Lecture (Monologue)	*J. Warner, MS*
Cricket Lightens	*Pat Cory*
Cricket Lovely Cricket (Up Spaghetti Junction)	*Jon Raven, 1973*
Cricket, Lovely Cricket (Victory Test Match Calypso)	*Egbert Moore*
Cricket Lyrics (some have had musical settings)	*T. Disney, 1897*
Cricket Mad (instrumental)	*Simon May*

(The) Cricket Man – humorous song	Fred Frampton, K. Prowse & Co, 1904
Cricket Master (voice and pfte.)	Betjeman, John Gould, 1976
(The) Cricket Match (pfte.)	Joyce Edginton, 1962, Hinricksen
Cricket Match	Charles Harrison, 1977
(The) Cricket Match (sung by The Singing Postman)	1966. Dick James Music
Cricket Match (the Village Cricket Match)	Smethurst, James Mus
(The) Cricket Match (No. 7 from Screen Fragments) – incidental music for pfte.	Peter Yorke, K. Prowse, 1938
Cricket Monologue	J. Warner
Cricket (Nottingham Quincentenary Pageant) – for full orchestra	L. du Garde Peach, William Summers 1949
Cricket on the Green	Arlott, The Yetties
Cricket on the Hearth	Norman Gale, Joseph Moorat, MS
Cricket on Tom Bowling (Burlesque Opera)	A. Hickman-Smith, 1939
Cricket on the Village Green	Cass, Myers, Grahame, 1966
Cricket on the Village Green	Bonny Sartin, 1979. White Hart Music
Cricket's Pink Ticket	Carney, Herbert, 1948
Cricket (Play it cool)	Gordon Franks
(The) Cricket Polka, pour piano	Emile Ettling, Robert Cocks
Cricket Samba	Legray, Moore, Shaftesbury
Cricket Song	R. G. Barlow, 1880
(A) Cricket Song on the Match when the Nottingham played the Sheffield and Leicester Clubs at Darnall. (Tune – Hey, Derry, Derry)	1826
Cricket Song	A. A. Brockington, Thomas Facer, J. Curwen & Sons
(The) Cricket Song (see Radnage Cricket Song)	arr. M. Campbell
Cricket Song	F. Edmonds, C. T. West, J. Curwen & Sons.

Cricket Songs (Apart from the four itemized separately, it is possible others from the volumes of songs by Gale have had musical settings.)	Norman Gale
Cricket Song (Tune — Drinking Song)	Celia Haddon, U.S.S.
Cricket (a song dedicated to A. N. Hornby)	J. Harcourt Smith, Wolverhampton, 1882
Cricket: the song of the 'Centurues'	J. Harcourt Smith, Howard & Co., 1895
Cricket Song (Ye Cricketers of England) (Tune — Ye Mariners of England)	Revd S. Hope. Dr Calcott
(A) Cricket Song and Elegy: John Smith	Abel Kidd, 'Old Stump', Highgate, 1873
Cricket Song (two part song)	P. La Villa, White-Smith Mus.
(The) Cricket Song	Lord Kitchener, Rupert Nurse and Orch.
Cricket Song (Tune — White Cockade)	Manea C.C., 1791
(A) Cricket Song (Songs of School Life)	Greville Matheson, James M. Gallatly, 1912, Weekes & Co.
Cricket Song	M. P. T., 1888, J. Williams
(The) Cricket Song (vocal with pfte.)	G. F. Martin, 1973
Cricket Song (Farjeon Reviewed)	Ken Moule
(A) Cricket Song: vocal march with chorus	A. A. Purry, G. Lishman, Novello & Chester, 1908
Cricket Song	L.E. Ridsdale, Alfred Hays
(A) Cricket Song	Clement Scott, c. 1894
(A) Cricket Song (Sedbergh School)	R. St. Ainslie, P. A. Thomas, Jackson, 1896
(The) Cricket Song	Geo. Alexander Stevens, 1740s.
Cricket Songs (Incl: The Beginning of the Season; Sing a Song of Cricketers; The End of the Season)	H. W. Timperley, Alan Dodson, 1941
Cricket Song (Uppingham)	E. Thring & C. Reimers

(A) Cricket Song	N. Wanostrocht 'Felix', 1864
Cricket Song (Tonbridge — Mathias and Strickland's School Songs, No. 12)	H. J.J. Watson, A. Herbert Brewer
Cricket Song	J. Wayne, Macmelodies
(A) Cricket Song (Manheim)	Grinnell Willis
Cricket Song	W.H.B.
Cricket Spring Song	Martineau and St. Claire, 1927, Dix Music
Cricket Theme	C. Washington, 1976, Chappell
Cricket Time	Francis Bosworth, Spin Publications
Cricket Umpires	A. Roberts, 1967
Cricket Umpiring	Sam Sklair
Cricket versus Golf (Concert Party Folio No. 12)	Reg Low, F. D. & H
Cricket Victory	Frank Holder, Palace Mus. 1976
Cricket World Cup	N. Khan, Peoples Culture Corps, 1977
(The) Cricketer (Air — 'Hearts of Oak')	
(The) Cricketer (see To live a life free from gout)	
(The) Cricketer (song) (at least 4 edtns)	W. J. Bullock (circa 1869) Weippert & Co.
(The) Cricketer (Union School Songs)	M. C. Gillington, F. Pascal, Jos. Williams
(The) Cricketers' ABC	Harry Syndey, 1862
(The) Cricketer's Alphabet for 1874	Abel Kidd, 'Old Stump'
(The) Cricketer's Carol	Sir Spencer Ponsonby-Fane H. Preston-Thomas, 1908
(The) Cricketers Club, a new song by an old hand	
Cricketers' Convention (Novelty No.)	Mena Silas
Cricketer's Dinner Song	Harry Sydney, 1862

(The) Cricketers' Galop with vocal chorus	Charles Denney, James Inglis & Sons
(A) Cricketer's Lament (suggested by a well-known song)	CHD., 1881
(The) Cricketers' National Song (A Choral March) (Dedicated to Dr. W.G.Grace)	F. Thomson, J. Curwen & Son
(The) Cricketer's Notebook by an old Cricketer	1882
(The) Cricketers of Hambledon	Bruce Blunt, Peter Warlock Augener, 1929
(The) Cricketers or the sports of Chapel-Town	A new dance, 1780
(The) Cricketer's Polka (small orchestra)	Peter Haysom
(The) Cricketer's Polka (introducing Airs from Masaniello)	R. W. Kohler, Ewer & Co.
(The) Cricketers Song	A. L. Cowley
(A) Cricketer's Song after the battle	
Cricketers' Song	E.G.M. G. A. Macfarren, 1857, Novello
Cricketers' Song (The Royal Game)	Wm. Flockton, Samuel Clark, 1895, J. Williams
(A) Cricketer's Song	Daniel H. C. Nelson, 1831, J. Chappell
(The) Cricketers' Song (dedicated to Jack Hobbs)	P. S. Robinson, 1934 Sylvester Music Co.
(The) Cricketers' Song (dedicated to W. G. Grace Esq.)	Francis Read & Stephen Stratton, Novello, Ewer & Co
(The) Cricketers' Song (A National Song)	Kent Sutton, Orpheus Music
(The) Cricketers' Song (Written on the occasion of the opening match of the Hastings Caxton C.C.)	Frank Thomson, A. Bertini & Co
Cricketers' Song (dedicated to Blue Mantles Club)	Julian Wright, A. Demain Grange, P. Derek, 1934
Cricketers' Supper Song	M. Lucien Boullemier, c. 1925
(The) Cricketers' Tent (a digest of cricketing facts and feats — A. Spectator, Esq.)	'Bat' F. Platts, 1863

Cricketing (Songs of Fives)	
Cricketing's all the rage. A new song	*Durham*
(The) Cricketing girls of '34 (Windmill Revnue)	*Burrows, Boyle*
Cricketing Horse (Musical Monologue)	*Kenneth Western, 1955*
The Death of the Ashby-de-la-Zouch C.C.: a song (Tune — Maggie Lawder)	*Beadmoores, 1827 Ashby*
Domestic Ditties	*A. Scott-Gatty Pearson 1901*
The Domum Galop	*J. G. Jones, Winchester*
The Double Match — an old song	*Rowland Colborn, A. G. Colborn Hart & Co. Paternoster Row*
Down went the wicket (Sung by T. H. Clark)	
Dreadlock Holiday (10 C.C.)	*E. Stewart, G. Gouldman, Mercury*
Duke of Norfolk	*Richard Stilgoe*
The Dungiven Cricket Match	*S.E.*
The Eleven of England, a cricketer's song (Sung by Mr Aislabie)	
England *v* West Indies, 1980	*Colin Shakespeare*
Establishment Blues (Mojo Singers)	*Allan Johnston & Alan Morris, W.E.A.*
Eton Songs:	
Cricket song (reissued as Cricket is King)	*A. C. Ainger & J. Barnby Novello*
Cricket song. Eton *v* Harrow.	*Swain 1864*
Eton *v* Epsom	*William Stone, 1814*
Eton and Harrow Valse by an Eton boy (ded. to C. I. Thornton Esq.)	*Ingalton-Drake*
Eton and Winchester: a song of the match	*R. T. Warner & F. S. Kelly Eton College Press, 1903*
Floreat Etona O.E. Lords, 1910	
Floreat Etona	*Nevill, 1911*
Floreat Etona.	*Parker*

A Song of Lord's, 1910	W. D. Eggar
Evening Song (Then fill a boglet)	Box
Every Day is a rainbow day for me (Not a cricket song but music by Don Bradman)	Words by Jack Lumsdaine
Fair Ilkley's ancient feast	1891
The Farmer	J. O'Keefe, 1800
The Fine Old English Cricketer. Tune — The Fine old English Gentleman. (Bat's Manual and Vincent's Pocket Companion)	
The Fine old English Game (Tune either — 'Highland Home' or 'The Fine old English Gentleman')	c. 1830
Fine weather, Fair cricket	
First in the Field	
Fitzalan-Howard	Richard Stilgoe
Floors Castle Cricketers Song (Tune — Dolly Dobbs)	
Floreat Cricket	Begley
Fontainbleau: a comic opera	J. O'Keefe, 1787
Football or Misery and Mud (Sung by W. F. Moss) (Contains verse on cricket)	Wal Pink, W. G. Eaton
Footer has fled (A Song of Cricket)	
For I ask ye again (Australian Song)	n.d.
Four Jolly Bowlers	Arlott, The Yetties, 1976
Gallinazo	P. I. Pieris, Ceylon
A Game at Cricket (Sports & Pastimes of the British Isles)	Ralph Alard. Orpheus Music Publishers
The Game of Cricket	Quondam cricketer of Kent, and Jacobus Junior
Games (School Union Song)	John E. Campbell, Lester Ralph. Novello & Co.
The Gentlemen's Cricketers' Team (A song, Wickets in the West)	
Getting up a side (Songs of sports and pastimes)	Cyril Stacy, 1937. Vinton
The Good Old Has-Beens (The Trentham C.C. song)	M. Lucien Boullemier c. 1925

Green Green Fields (parody of 'The Green Green Grass of home')	*Max Boyce, 1979*
Hail and Farewell (Tonbridge School)	*Clemence Dane, Thomas Wood, 1921*
Harold Gimblett's Hundred (Five slightly different versions)	*Arlott, The Yetties, 1975*

Harrow School Songs:

Awake	*E.E.B. & E.F., 1886*
Byron lay	*E.E.B. & J.F., 1884*
F.P.	*E.E.B., 1895*
A Gentleman's a-bowling	*E. E. Bowen & Eaton Faning, 1888*
Giants	*E.E.B. & J.F., 1874*
The Harrow Alphabet, 1864	
If time is up	*E.E.B. & E.F., 1895*
Jack and Joe	*E.E.B. & J.F., 1876*
Lord's 1873	*E.E.B.*
Lord's 1878	*E.E.B.*
Lord's 1900	*E.E.B.*
The niner	*E.E.B. & E.F., 1887*
'Queen Elizabeth sat one day'	*E.E.B. & J.F., 1875*
R.G.	*E.E.B., 1884*
Stet Fortuna Domus (cricketing verse for 1891)	*E. W. Howson & E.F., 1891*
Willow the King (dedicated to Hons. R. Grimston & F. Ponsonby)	*E. E. Bowen, John Farmer Duke & Sons, 1867*

Have a go	*A. Johnston, A. Morris, Warner Bros Music*
Hawks and Doves (American Cricket)	*Richard Stilgoe*
Her was the prettiest fellow (The Richmond Heiress 1693. Slightly different version in Pills to Purge Melancholy 1698)	*Thomas D'Urfey*

Here come the Aussies (Penny Farthing) (Australian Cricket Team 1972)	Daniel Boone, Rod McQueen
Here's to Lascelles Hall	E. A. Lodge
The High Catch	Arlott, The Yetties, 1976
The Holiday Quadrille (based on popular melodies) (front cover includes cricketing theme)	Stephen Glover, Robert Cocks & Co.
The Honorary Colonel's Song (with apologies to W. S. Gilbert)	1899
How McDougal topped the Score (has had folk accompaniment)	Thomas E. Spencer
How's that (sung by T.E. Dunville)	Worton David & Shirley Ilton, Reeder Walsh
How's that? — Well caught: a comic song	London, n.d.
Howzat (sung by Sherbet)	G. Porter, T. Mitchell, Epic
The hunt of the leather (dedicated to A. C. Oddie Esq., Sussex C.C.C.)	J. St Clair E. Harold Melling, Bach & Co., 1912
Hurrah! for the noble game of cricket (Opera: She Stoops to Conquer)	E. Fitzball, G. A. Macfarren, 1863
I keep it there or thereabouts	Arlott, The Yetties, 1977
I'm rather too old for it now	Charles Coborn, Charles Sheard
I seem not to care (*see* Song of the Cricketer)	'Bats' Manual
I sing the song of Ilkley	John Ramsbotham, 1894
I Zingari Galop (dedicated to the members of the I Zingari Club)	Henry Brosang, J. Wiseheart
I Zingari Polka	Clindon
I Zingari Song (Tune — Red, White and Blue)	W. Bolland
John Brown's Body parody (Dartford C.C.)	1931
The Jolly Cricket Ball	C.M. & E. G. Monk, c. 1850 Novello
The Josser Cricketer (The True Story of a Test Match)	Mark Sheridan, F.D.H.
The Josser's Cricket Club (sung by Herbert Campbell)	W. B. Eaton, F. Bowyer

The Jovial Cricketers	*1776*
The Kentish Cricketer	*c. 1815*
Kerry Packer	*Richard Stilgoe*
King Cricket	*A. B. Cooper, E. Markham Lee 1895. J. Curwen*
Lancashire (More songs and snatches)	*Perceval Graves, 1977*
The last rose of summer (parody)	
Lawyers out of mischief (Burhill Park, Esher)	*1857*
Life is like a game of cricket	*Frank Hall, Duff & Stewart, c. 1870*
Lilian Thomson	*Richard Stilgoe*
Little Boxes (sung by Fred Wedlock)	
Long-on-Blues	*Farjeon*
London will be the same	*Bill Stephens and Peter Akister*
Lord's Pavilion (sung by Instant Sunshine)	*Peter Christie*
Married *v* Single (with apologies to Mr. W. S. Gilbert)	*C.P.*
M.C.C. *v* W. Indies	*Lord Beginner & his Caribbean Calypso Band*
The Marylebone ranks first of all (Tune – Rule Britannia)	
Merion Club Song (Tune – Heidelberg)	
The Merry Athletes March	*Wymark Stratton, Bowerman & Co.*
The Merry Cricketers' Polka (dedicated to St. John's C.C.)	*R. Desanges. Rudall, Rose, and Carte*
Middlesex *v* Bucks	*William Wilson, 1864*
Mr Aislabie's Song	*1833*
Mohammedan Song	
My Cricket Girl (a vocal novelty)	*Frank Leo, F.D. & H., 1903*
My friends leave your work	*Baxter, Lewes*
Mystery of B.B.	*Brother 'Brewer'*

The National Game of Old England. (Tune – The Union Jack of England)	
Northamptonshire C.C.C. song. (Tune – Bonny Dundee)	*J. P. Kingston, 1885*
No Spanish Don	*Joseph Moorat, MS*
Now this new kind of cricket (Our Miss Gibbs) (Extra verse added by Cyril Ritchard)	
The O.B's Battle Song	*C. Armstrong Gibbs, R. Straus, E. Gillett*
Obstruction (Ruthless Rhymes for Heartless Homes)	*E. Arnold, V. Hely-Hutchinson, Elkin, 1945*
Ode: Fifty years have sped (Oxford v Cambridge)	*C. S. Bere, 1851*
Oh, Sackville, Richmond, Tankerville (Closer)	*Richard Stilgoe*
Oh, the Sheffielders	*A local poet, 1870*
Old Boys All (Tonbridge School)	*Clemence Dane, Thomas Wood, 1921*
Old Boys Match: Amersham Hall School	*Ernest Radford*
The Old Boys Match (Uppingham School)	*E. Thring, W. Richter, 1887*
The Old English Cricketer	
The Old English Cricketer	*Mr. Ffinch, Secretary, Blackheath (Dartmouth) C.C.*
On Surrey Hills (Banstead School Song)	*J. M. Bastard, Orton Bradley Jos. Williams Ltd.*
On the Game of Cricket	*J.J.B.*
On the Spot	*Norman Gale*
The Origins of cricket	*Richard Digance*
The Origin of the Kennington Union C.C. written and sung by the President of the Club	
Our Cricket Song	*J.J.R., 1893*
Our Don Bradman	*Jack O'Hagan, Allan & Co., 1930*
Our Eleven	*Jack Lumsdaine, D. Davis & Co., 1930*

Out (sung by Fred Harvey)	*Charles Wilmott, Fred Eplett. B. Mocatta & Co.*
Ow's that? (Songs of sports and pastimes)	*Cyril Stacy 1937 Vinton*
Oxford Joe	*Frank W. Green & J. Harrington Young. London, C. Sheard*
A Paean of Triumphal Rhymes	*1831*
Peace, Peace (Rajah of Bhong) — A Country Girl	*Monckton, Ross, Rubens, Greenbank*
The Pelican Lancers (dedicated to the Boys of The Pelican Club)	*arr. by Edward Solomon*
Pelican Polka (dedicated to The Pelican Club)	*Edward Solomon*
Phyllis at the wicket (More Songs and Snatches)	*Perceval Graves, 1977*
Play the Game	*Maurice Scott*
Play the Game (Jig-Saw Revue)	*F. W. Chappelle*
Play up, and play the game	
A Policeman's lot (parody) (Sharps and Flats) *See also* Sergeant's song	*Donald Douglas, 1929*
The Prerogative of Pipers' Flat	*Thos. E. Spencer*
Prince of Wales	*Richard Stilgoe*
The race for the Championship in 1883	
Rachel Heyhoe (Tune — Banana Boat Song)	*Richard Stilgoe*
The Radnage Cricket Song (collected by H. Harman)	*trad. arr. M. Campbell*
Ranji: new song	*C. T. West, Brighton, Lyon & Hall, c. 1895*
Ranjitsinghji Waltz	*Charles T. West, Weekes & Co.*
The Rape of Helen: a mock opera	*J. Breval, 1737*
Raspberry Time in Runcorn (On with the Dance)	*Noel Coward, 1923 A.H. & C.*
Red is Red (Sung by F. Trueman)	
The Return (Booth Song — Uppingham)	*E. Thring, P. David, 1877*

The Right Cricketer	*Amy Mortimer, E. V. Lucas, MS.*
The Roedean XI	
Roll on the Covers (sung by Instant Sunshine)	*Peter Christie*
Round-Hand Bowling	*Du Terreaux, Alberto Randegger*
Rub it in	*Joseph Moorat, Norman Gale, MS.*
Run, run, run, the ball's a rolling (Tune — Tramp, Tramp, Tramp)	*H. Hutchinson*
The School Cricket Song (Northern Congregational School)	*P. J. Wood, W. F. Kelvey, Wakefield, 1902*
School of our Fathers	*Ceylon*
See the Cricketers of Kent	*J. Burnby, S. Porter, 1825*
Sergeant's Song (Pirates of Penzance) — parody	*Gilbert & Sullivan*
The Seasons Galop	*W. Smallwood, Brewer & Co.*
She didn't know enough about the game (The Silver Slipper)	*G. Rollit and L. Stuart F & D.*
Shrewsbury Songs:	
The changes of a year have shed (Tune – The Girl I Left behind me)	*Anon. 1869*
Full many a changing year (Time – The Girl I left behind me)	*Various Old Boys, 1873*
If you'll give me your attention (Tunes from 'Princess Ida')	*Rev. W. A. W. Evans, 1884*
If you want to hear a ditty (Tune from 'Patience')	*Rev. W. A. W. Evans, 1882*
I have a song to sing oh! (Tune from 'The Yeomen of the Guard')	*Rev. W. A. W. Evans, 1889*
I have gazed, dear friends, on the altered face (Tune – 'Trial by Jury')	*Owen Seaman 1885*
I'll sing you a song (Tune – 'The Meynell Hunt')	*Rev. W. A. W. Evans, 1892*
Lord 'dowled' me to sing (Tune from 'The Gondoliers')	*Rev. W. A. W. Evans, 1890*
The Old Boy's Song (Tune from 'Ivanhoe')	*Rev. W. A. W. Evans, 1891*

There is a very good old song (Tune – A Fine Old English Gentleman.'	*E. G. Hall, 1872*
Up Forward all, and Onward all (Tune – original by Rev. E.G. Hall)	*Rev. E .G. Hall, 1888*
A welcome to you all (Tune from 'The Mikado')	*H. K. St. John Sanderson, 1886*
We take him from the 'crammer' or the 'coach' (Tune – Tommy Atkins)	*Rev. W. A. W. Evans, 1894*

Sing Muse the Man	*Baxter*
Sing a Song of Haileybury	*1898*
Sing Willow	*Farjeon*
Singing up P.I.P.I.P.I. (Tune — Singing Ay Ay Yippy Yippy Ay)	*Ceylon*
The Sky-Lark: a collection of English songs	
Slowman's Chant (Teignbridge C.C.)	*G. Templer*
Snow in the West Indies	*Richard Stilgoe*
Soldiers of the Willow	*G. E. Evans, Alberto Zelman Allan & Co.*
Somerset C.C. Song	*M. J. 'Bonnie' Sartin Maypole Music*
Song at the end of the great Cricket Week by a Canterbury Belle	
Song of the Bat	*The Alleynian, Dulwich College, 1901*
Song of the County Championship	
A Song of Cricket	*D. L. A. Jephson, A. H. Behrend. Weekes, 1919*
Song of the Cricketer (I seem not to care) (Two versions)	*'Bat'. Thirlwall, Meyer Lutz, 1850*
The Song of the Emeriti	*Capt. C. Welman, L. Wheeler Esq. F.D. & H. 1878*
Song of the English Cricketers (Tune — Bonny Dundee)	*Mr Lyon. Truedel & Co.*
The Song of the fast bowler (Tune — Canadian Boat Song 'Row, brothers, Row')	

Song of the Games (Wycombe)	
Song of the Kaffir	
Song of Life	*A. K. Gaul, 1892*
Songs of the bat	*E. V. Lucas, 1892*
Songs of the Cricket Field	*F. C. Benson, 1932*
Songs in Solitude	*Hill*
Songs of sports and pastimes	*Cyril Stacy, 1937*
Soul Limbo	*Booker T. and the M.Gs.*
Sparkling	*Joseph Moorat, Norman Gale, MS.*
Sporting Girls	*C. Deane, F.D. & H.*
Sports Galop for the pianoforte	*S. Vizentini, Duff & Stewart*
The Sportsman (verse 3)	*Arthur Askey, Robert Rutherford*
Sports and Pastimes (Humorous Song or Concerted Item)	*Noel Pherns and Jennifer Gwyn*
Sticky Wicket blues	*Jonathan Adams*
Stonewall Jack	*Arlott, The Yetties, 1979*
Success to the friends of the bat and the ball. *See* Song of the cricketer (I seem not to care)	
Sunshine (recorded by The Spinners)	*Leslie Haworth, Fontana*
A Sussex welcome to the Wanderers (Tune — Oh Willie we have missed you)	
The Taverners Song	*Percy S. Robinson, MS.*
Temperance Songs for Elder Children (One is a cricketing song)	*E. Cympson*
That's not cricket (At Home Abroad) (Sung by Eleanor Powell)	*Dietz, Schwarz, 1935, Chappell & Co.*
Then fill a goblet (Song of the Cricketer) (Bat's Manual 1851) *See* Evening Song	*Box*
There's an animal Test Match (Rebecca of Sunnybrook Farm)	*1932/3*
There's the cricketers bold	*Mr Beind, 1863*

Thomians Young and Thomians Old	
The Tie Match, a new comic song (Tune — Trab, Trab)	*J. D. Mills, 1852*
To a Chucker (Songs of sports and pastimes)	*Cyril Stacy, 1937 Vinton*
To the Kilkenny Cricket Club	*1831*
To live a life free from gout (The Cricketer) (Sportsmans Vocal Cabinet — Charles Armiger)	*1831*
The Treats of London, a comic descriptive song	*J. Fairburn, 1815*
The Trueman Calypso (sung by Ronnie Hilton)	
Two hundred years of cricket	*Richard Stilgoe*
Ulyett's L.B.W.	*Richard Stilgoe*
The Umpire (dedicated to A. G. Steel)	*Noss Mayo. E. Donajouraki, 1890*
Up at Lord's (Songs of School Life)	*Greville Matheson, Francis Thorns, Weeks & Co. 1914*
Upgreen and at 'em or a Maiden nearly over, a cricketing melodrama with music.	*Ray Terry, 1960*
Uppingham School Song	*E. Thring, P. David.*
Valse I Zingari	*A. D. Porter, Metzler & Co.*
The Veterans' Song (with apologies to W. S. Gilbert)	*F. C. M. Richards*
The Vexed Bowler (Tune — The gay cavalier)	*J. D. Mills, 1853*
The Fexed Bowler (The English Game of Cricket, Box)	*1860*
Victor Trumper (Bush ballads)	*Guy Eden*
Village Cricket (sung by Instant Sunshine)	*Peter Christie*
The Village Match	*Richard Elton*
The Village Rondo	*Matthias von Holst, 1812-15*
The Village Team	*Richard Elton*
Vitae Lampada	*Henry Newbolt*
Vivat Haileyburia	
We got Thommo	*Smith & Weston, Wayne Roberts, RCA. 1975*
What's a Pommie (sung by Rolf Harris)	*Don Spencer, Cinephonic*

When an old cricketer leaves the crease	*Roy Harper, E.M.I.*
When cricket first in olden time (Clarke's song)	
When the meadows are aglow (More Songs and Snatches)	*Perceval Graves, 1977*
'When wacker broke the window', set to music by 'Boozey'	
The White Willow Tree	*Leno*
Who's Grovelling now (calypso) (Sung by Ezeike)	*Jama*
'Will you bowl a little faster' said the Dodo to the Gnurk (Cricket through the Looking-Glass)	*Whimsical Song. R. C. Robertson — Glasgow*
Willow is the wood for me (Unison School Songs)	*M. C. Gillington, F. Pascal Joseph Williams*
Willow the King	*Herbert Farjeon, Michael Sayer*
Women's Recruiting Song (reference to cricket) (*See* 'Your King and Country')	
A wonderful joy our eyes to bless (Utopia Ltd.)	*Gilbert & Sullivan*
Ye famous battel of Trent Bridge (Tune — Ye Bailiff's Daughter of Islington)	
Your King and Country Want You (A Woman's Recruiting Song) (ref. to cricket)	*Paul A. Rubens Pub. Chappell & Co.*
Zingari Galop (dedicated to Zingari C.C.)	*Karl Meyder Chappell & Co.*
Zingari March: two step	*Theron D. Perkins, Jean White, Boston 1897*
Zummerzet varsus Zurrey (Reprinted from *Somerset County Gazette*, 22 August 1891)	*A. P. Graves, 1891*

Credits

The authors and publishers are grateful to the following for permission to reproduce copyright material (where applicable) in this book

Come all to Stoolball D'Urfey, Pills to Purge Melancholy; *The Cricket Song* trad. collected by Horace Harman (Buckinghamshire dialect), Blandford Press, 1954; *Cricket Song* (White Cockade), Frederick Lillywhite cricket scores and biographies, volume 1; *The Village Rondo* Matthias von Holst, Bland and Wellers Music Warehouse; *Brown of Brighton* John Arlott, The Yetties, unpublished; *See the Cricketers of Kent* J Burnby, S Porter, W Dale, Poultry, London; *The Darnall Cricket Song* reproduced from an original broadside, Nottinghamshire Cricket and Cricketers by F S Ashley-Cooper, Henry B Saxton, Nottingham, 1923; *The Death of the Ashby-de-la-Zouch Cricket Club* Beadsmoores, Printers, Ashby, 1827; *Lawyers out of Mischief* Feltham's Cricketer for 1877; *The Cricketer* Sportsman's Vocal Cabinet, Charles Arminger, T Griffiths; *The Cricketer's Song* Daniel H C Nelson, J Chappell, Royale Exchange, 1831; *Kickenny Cricket Song* privately printed; *A Cricket song* Samuel R Hole, privately printed by Richards, Nottingham (1922); *Clarke's Song* Nottinghamshire Cricket and Cricketers by F S Ashley-Cooper, Henry B Saxton, Nottingham (1923); *The I Zingari Song* William Bolland, The Canterbury Cricket Week; *The I Zingari Galop* Henry Brosang, J. Wisehart, Jnr.; *Zingari Galop* Karl Mayder, Chappell & Co.; *'Zingari' March* Theron D Perkins, Boston (Mass) Jean White (1897); *Valse I Zingari* A D Porter, M. Gunn & Sons; *Cricket* Harry and Leo Trevor, Alfred Scott-Batty, Boosey & Co; *Success to the Friends of the Bat and the Ball* Thirlwall; *The Vexed Bowler* J D Mills, Wandsworth; *Cricketing's all the Rage* broadsheet; *The Cricketers' Galop* Charles Denney, James Inglis & Sons; *Cricket Song* R G Barlow; *Cricket, The Song of the Centuries* J Harcourt-Smith, Howard & Co 1895; *Cricket after Grace* Harry Adams, Howard & Co, Felix Dumas, F D & H; *The Cricketers* Kent Sutton, Orpheus Music Publishing Co., 1896; *The Cricket Bat Polka* Henry A Sutch, Chas. Shread & Co.; *Cricketers Song* William Flockton. Samuel E Clark, Joseph Williams, 1895; *Cricket* H G L Mills, Edmund Forman, 1889; *Ranji* Charles T West, Lyon and Hall, Brighton; *Ranjitsinhj Waltz* Charles T West, Weekes & Co.; *A Sussex Welcome to the Wanderer* 'Cricket' magazine 1899; *R Abel, Surrey* A Craig, Penny sheet; *Zummerzet versus Zurrey* A P Graves, Woodley & Co. Taunton; *The Song of the Emeriti* Captain C Welman, Francis Bros & Day (1878); *Life Is Like A Game of Cricket* Frank Hall, Duff and Stewart (c. 1870); *Cricketers Supper Song* L Boullemier, Trentham (c. 1925); *The Northamptonshire Cricket Song* J P Kingston MS (1885); *The Cricketer* W J Bullock, Weippert & Co. (c. 1869); *Sparkling* Norman Gale, Methuen & Co., 1894; *No Spanish Don* set to music by Joseph Moorat; *Advice Gratis* Norman Gale/Ellis Wynne, Wright & Co.; *The Right Cricketer* E V Lucas, A E Mortimer, MS; *The Australian XI Galop* Charles Pratt, W.H.Glen & Co., Melbourne; *Australian Cricketers' Chorus* (Pot-Pouri, 1899 Review), W H Risque; *Soldiers of the Willow* Evans and Zelman, Allan and Co., Melbourne; *Song of the English Cricketers* Mr Lyon; *Down went the Wicket* Rowland and A G.Colborn, Hart and Co., Paternoster Row; *The Boy's Cricket Song* Sam Walton, Edmonton, Canada; *The Cricket and the Bat, A Natural History Match in Three Innings and a Musical Score* Harry Gifford, Alf J Lawrence, 1914, F D & H; *The O.B. Song* Armstrong Gibbs, Ralph Straus, Eric Gillett, Favel Press; *The Good Old Has-Beens* L Boullemier, Trentham (c.1925); *Cricket Spring Song* G D Martineau/Dix Music (1927); *The Cricketers of Hambledon* Peter Warlock, Bruce Blunt, Augener, 1929. *Our Eleven* Jack Lumsdaine, D Davis & Co., Sydney; *Ev'ry Day is Rainbow Day for Me* Jack Lumsdaine, Don Bradman, D Davis & Co., Sydney; *Our Don Bradman* Jack O'Hagan, Allan & Co., Melbourne; *The Cricketers' Song* P S Robinson. Sylvester Music Co., 1934; *Harold Gimbletts Hundred* John Arlott; *The Cricketers Song* A Demain Grange/J Wright. Peter Derek Ltd.; *Sing a Song of Cricketers* H W Timperley. Alan Dodson. *Cricket Song* R St. J Ainslie, Leeds, Jackson & Sedbergh, 1896; *The Northern Congregational School Cricket Song* P J Wood, Wakefield (1902); *Cricketing Song* E Cympson. Temperance Songs for Elder Children (c. 1879); *Up at Lords* G E Matheson, Francis Thorn, Weekes Co.; *On Surrey Hills* J M Bastard/Orton Bradley. Joseph Williams Ltd.; *The Cricketer* Pascal and Gillington. Joseph Williams; *Round Hand Bowling* Du Terreaux and Randegger; *Cricket Song (Tonbridge)* Herbert Brewer, Matthias & Strickland's School Songs; *The Old Boys' Match* E Thring. Uppingham School Songs. T Fisher Unwin; *The Domum Galop* J G Jones. Winchester; *Eton and Winchester* F S Kelly, R T Warner. Eton College Press, 1903; *Cricket is King* A C Ainger/J Barnby, Simpson, Marshall, Kent & Novello; *Eton v Harrow Valse* Eton old boy; *Willow the King* E E Bowen, J Farmer. Cassell. Duke and Co.; *A Gentleman's a-bowling* E E Bowen, E Faning (1888);

The Niner E E Bowen, E Faning. Novello & Co.; *If Time is Up* E E Bowen, E Faning, (1889). Novello & Co.; *Song of the Games* Gaudeamus Songs – Farmer's collection. Cassell; *Cricket Verse (Roedean)* Nancy Spain. Noel Coward Estate. *Raspberry Time in Runcorn (On with the Dance)* Noel Coward. Samuel French. Noel Coward Estate; *The Treats of London* J Fairburn 1815. Epilogue spoken at play (Gentlemen Cricketers of Barrow). Cricketing references in Norwich Newspapers 1701-1800, J S Penny. Norwich 1979; *A Cricketers Prologue* Tom Taylor: *Come Listen all Good People* Mr Hartopp; *The Cricketing Songs* Harry Sydney, 1862; *Hurrah Hurrah for the Noble Game of Cricket* E Fitzball, G Macfarren. Cramer, Wood & Co.; *What Means This Paper Warfare* Clara Denvil; *A Cricket Song* Grinnell Willis. American Cricketer, 1892; *A Wonderful Joy Our Eyes To Bless* (Utopia Ltd) Chappells, Gilbert and Sullivan. *The Jossers' Cricket Club* F Bowyer/W G Eaton. H & C; *The Josser Cricketer* Mark Sheridan, F D & H; *The Cricket-Man* Fred Frampton. K Prowse & Co., 1904; *My cricket Girl* Frank Leo. F D & H. *How's that* Worton David, Shirley Ilton, Reeder & Walsh, 1906; *Peace, Peace* Ross, Greenbank, Rubens; *The Taverners' Song* P S Robinson. Unpublished; *The Captain of the Prison Cricket Team* Bob Halfin, Harold Irving; *Roll on the covers* Peter Christie. Unpublished; *Lords Pavilion* Peter Christie, unpublished; *Cricket Lovely Cricket* Egbert Moore. Melodisc Ltd; *The Cricket Song* Aldwyn Roberts, EMI; *Cricket Calypso* David Henry Wilson, 1980; *Lilian Thomson* Richard Stilgoe. *200 Years of Cricket* Richard Stilgoe. Noel Gay Music Ltd; *Sticky Wicket Blues* Jonathan Adams; *Little Boxes* Fred Wedlock; *The High Catch* John Arlott/The Yetties; *A Tickle a' me Spinning Finger* John Arlott/The Yetties; *Somerset C C C* M J Sartin. Maypole Music; *Lancashire* Percival Graves, Dunstable Litho; *Sunshine* L Haworth, 'Spinners' Fontana L P; *Cricket – The Vicar* (The Kinks), R D Davies, Davray Music; *Green Green Fields* Max Boyce Songbook, Weidenfeld; *And Did Those Feet* Bruce Ogston. Unpublished; *The Ashes Song 70-71* Vic Lewis. Ken Thorne; *Here come the Aussies* Boone. McQueen, Penny Farthing Records; *C'mon Aussie C'mon* A Johnston/A Morris. Warner Brothers Music; *When An Old Cricketer Leaves the Crease* Roy Harper (c) Great Western Myths Ltd/Blackhill Music Ltd. Recorded on Roy Harper album 'HQ', EMI SHVL.

Every effort has been made to contact the copyright owners but in some cases this has not been possible; any omissions that are notified to the publishers will be included in future editions.

Illustrations are reproduced by permission of the following: British Library page 16; Anthony Baer Collection at Melbourne Cricket Ground pages 29, 32, 43, 47, 61 (bottom), 65, 119; Valerie Harris page 153; Lord's Library pages 22, 30, 50, 75, 110, 111, 112, 113, 114, 115, 116, 117; John McKenzie page 187; Patrick Mullins 67, 87, 88; Sedbergh School Library 97, 98, 99, 100, 101, 102; Trustees of the Noel Coward Estate 128, 129; Anthony Winder 24, 25, 33, 40, 142, 143, 144. The illustrations on pages 48, 53, 80, 81, 82, 83, 84, 134 and 159 are from the author's collection. The illustrations were photographed by Joe Coomber with the exception of those in the Anthony Baer collection which were photographed by Patrick Eagar. The drawings on pages 4, 27 and 131 are from *English Sporting Prints* by James Laver published by Ward Lock Ltd; that on page 39 is from *England versus Australia* by David Frith published by Lutterworth Press; the illustrations on pages 58 and 85 are by Dennis Mallet from *Herbert Farjeon's Cricket Bag* published by Macdonald & Co.

Index

Page numbers in *italics* refer to illustrations

Abel, Bob 50, 54-5, 151
Able, R. 157
Adams, Jonathan 175
Adams, H. 48
ADVICE GRATIS (Gale) 62
Africa, South 78, 183
Ainger, Arthur Campbell 120
Ainslie, R. St. J. 96
Aistabie, Benjamin 26
Alberts, W. 157
ALL IN THE WRONG 12
Allahakbarries, The 74
Allan's, Messrs. 89
Allen, Frank 64, *65*
Allom, Maurice 184
Alresford C.C. 14
Amiss, D. 173
AND DID THOSE FEET (Ogston) 181-2
Andrew, Keith 164
Andrews, Bill 93
Arlott, John 17-18, 92, 164, 174, 176
Armiger, Charles 21
Arnold, E.G. 68, 70
AROUND THE FIELD AT HAVERFORD (Paine) 145
Artillery Ground, London 132
Asche, Oscar 160
Ashby-de-la-Zouch C.C. 22
ASHES SONG, THE 183
Assist all ye muses, and join to rehearse 12
At Home Abroad 162
Atom Bowler, The 164
Australia 31, 52, 64, *65*, 66, 68, 78, 86, 89, 141, *142-4*, 146, 149, 160-1, 163, 172-4, 183-4
AUSTRALIAN CRICKETERS' CHORUS (Risque) 66
AUSTRALIAN ELEVEN GALOP (Pratt) 64, *65*
Ayckbourn, Alan 162
Ayer, Nat. D. 160
Aylward, J. *80*

Baden-Powell, Robert 105
Baby Bunting 160
Bacchus, F. 171
Badgers Green 161

Bailey, George 64, *65*
Baker, T. 131
Baldwin, J.Loraine 28
Bannerman, Alec & Charles 64, *65*
Banstead School 106
Barber, 19
Barker, 20
Barlow, Richard Gorton 44
Barnby, Sir Joseph 120
Barrable, G.H. 31
Barrie, Sir James 74, 149
Barrow, Suffolk 131
Bassett, Willie 157
Bastard, J.M. 106
Bath 75-6
Batley C.C. 42
Batsman's Bride, The 164
Battcock, Oliver 162
Bax, Sir Arnold 74, 76
Bax, Clifford 74-6
Baxter, George 24
Baxter, 'Honest' 25
Baxter, John 24-5
Beckett, K.L. à 86
Bedser, Alec 164, 168
Beecham, Thomas 185
BEGINNING OF THE SEASON, THE (Timperley) 95
Behrend, A.H. 54
Beldham, William *80*
Bennett, G. *143-4*
Benson, Frank 146
Bignall, 140
Bimshaw '73 163
Birmingham Theatre Royal 135
Bishopsbourne Park, Kent 12
Bit of a Test, A 161
BITTER BEER 59
Black, Jay & Stephen 164
Blackham, John 31, 64, *65*
Blair, L. 164
Blue Mantles C.C. 94-5
Blunt, Bruce 79, *80-4*, 85
Blythe, Colin 184
Boddey, Martin 163
Bohemians, The 146
Bolland, William 27-8, 31, 136
Bonnor, G.J. 176
Boosey & Hawkes 90
Bosanquet, B.J.T. 68-9

Boullemier, Lucien 76
Boult, Sir Adrian 118
Bowen, Edward Ernest 120-1, *123*, 125, 127
BOWL A BALL, SWING A BAT 183
Bowman, 131
Boxall, T. 25
BOY'S CRICKET SONG, THE (Von Tilzer) 73
Boyce, Max 181
Boycott, Geoff 185-6
Boyle, Henry 64, *65*
Boyle, Paul 162
Box, Charles ('Bat') 40-1
Bradley, Orton 106
Bradman, Sir Don 86, 89
Brampton, 140
Braund, L.C. 68, 70
Brearley, Mike 174, 185
Brett, *80*
Breval, J. 131
Brighton, 17-18, 50, *51*, 72, 138, 140
Brisley, R.C. 159
Britcher, Samuel 12
Brockwell, W. 55
Brosang. Henry 29
Broughtonians, Old 74-6
Brown, George 17-18, 138
Brown of Brightelmstone's Ball (Browne) *17*, 17-18
Browne, Royman 17
Browne, Thomas 162
Brunswick records 184
Bullock, W.J. 59, *61*
Burgess, Bill 71
Burhill Park, Esher 23
Burnby, J. 19
Burnett, 23
Burrows, Rex 162
Burrup, 140-1, *143-4*
Butler, Dr. H. Montagu 121
Butterworth, George 118
Byron, G.F. 106

C'MON AUSSIE, C'MON C'MON 184
Caesar, Julius 79
Caffyn, William *143-4*
Calloway, T. 157
calypsos 167-72
Cambridge 62, 107, 118, 134,

211

136, 139, 184
Campbell, Madeleine 14
Canada 64, 72-3
Canterbury 12, 28, 31, 39, 136, 146
CAPTAIN OF THE PRISON CRICKET TEAM, THE (Halfin) 164
Carlo, 159
Casey, S. 159
Cassell & Co. Ltd. 121, *123*
Casson, Frank H. 72
Castle, Dennis 162
Cates, F. 159
Chappell, G. 174, 184
Chatteris C.C. 15
Chester's Messrs. 49
Chivers, Cedric 76
CHORUS OF THE SAND-WICH MEN, THE (Risque) 66
Christiani, R.J. 168
Christie, Campbell 162
circuses and cricket 146
Clark, Graham 164
Clark, T.H. 72-3
Clark, William Mark 27
Clarke, William 27-8, 59, *61*
Clarke, 20
Cobbett, W. 157
Coke, R. 170
Colborn, A.G. 73
Colborn, Rowland 73
Colman, George (snr. & junr.) 134, 136
COME ALL TO STOOL-BALL (Purcell) 11
Come Live With Me 162
Comic New Year's Budget of Songs 135
Common, Bob 177
Constanduras, Denis 164
Conway, John 64, *65*
Cotton, Rev. Reynell 12-13, 164
COTTON'S CRICKET SONG 12
Coward, Sir Noel 128
Cowdrey, Colin 107
Craig, Albert 54
Craig, Eddie 184-5
Cricket; an Heroic Poem 132
CRICKET (Mills) 49
CRICKET (Trevor) *34, 35-8*
CRICKET AFTER GRACE OR OUT! OUT! OUT! (Adams) 46, *48*
CRICKET AND CALYPSO 165

Cricket and Cricketers 131
CRICKET AND WIMBLEDON 165
Cricket at Sea 63
CRICKET BAT POLKA, THE (Sutch) 47
CRICKET CALYPSO, A (Wilson) 170-2
Cricket Comicalities and Football Oddities 141
CRICKET GROUND QUARTET, THE 165
CRICKET IN NOVEMBER (Grey) 160
CRICKET IS KING (Eton) 120
Cricket Match, The 164
CRICKET ON THE HEARTH (Gale) 60
CRICKET ON THE VILLAGE GREEN (Sartin) 177-8
CRICKET MUSIC DEALER *10*
CRICKET POLKA (Ettling) 56
CRICKET '76 (Coke) 170
CRICKET SONG (Barlow) 44
CRICKET SONG (Sedbergh) *97-102*
CRICKET SONG, A (Sheffield) 19-20
CRICKET SONG, A (Willis) 145
CRICKET SONG, THE (Lord Kitchener) 170
CRICKET SPRING SONG (Martineau) 78-9
cricket songs: historical development 9-96
CRICKET – THE SONG OF THE 'CENTURIES' (Smith) 44, *45*
CRICKET, THE VICAR 179
Cricket v. Golf 162
CRICKET-MAN, THE (Frampton) 150, *152*
CRICKETER, THE 21
CRICKETER, THE (Bullock) 59-60, *61*
CRICKETER, THE (Williams) 106
Cricketers, The (a dance) *133,* 134
CRICKETERS, THE (Sutton) 49
CRICKETERS' ABC, THE *144*
CRICKETERS CAROL,

THE (Ponsonby-Fane) 28
CRICKETERS CLUB, THE 26
CRICKETERS' DINNER SONG 143
CRICKETERS' GALOP, THE (Denney) 42, *43*
Cricketer's Manual 40, 41
CRICKETER'S NATIONAL SONG, THE (Thomson) 46
CRICKETERS OF HAMBLEDON, THE (Warlock) 79, *80-4,* 85
CRICKETER'S PROLOGUE, A 136-8
CRICKETER'S SONG (Macfarren) 139
CRICKETER'S SONG, THE (Nelson) 21
CRICKETER'S SONG, THE (Robinson) 90, *91*
CRICKETER'S SONG, THE (Wright) 95
CRICKETERS' SUPPER SONG 58
CRICKETING GIRLS OF 1934 (Burrows) 162
Cricketing Songs, The 142-4
CRICKETING'S ALL THE RAGE 42
Croft, Colin 171
Curwen, J. & Sons 46, 49
Cutmore, James 93, 184

D'Urfey, Thomas 11-12, 130-1
Daft, Richard 140
Daniel, John 92
Darling, Joe 66
Darnall cricket ground 19-20
Dartford C.C. 94
David, Worton 155, *156*
Davis, Tom B. 159
Davis, 19
Dawson, Forbes 148
DEATH OF THE ASHBY-DE-LA-ZOUCH CRICKET CLUB, THE 22
Dench, 'Little' 18
Denney, Charles 42, *43*
Dennis, 19
Dewar, T.R. *158,* 159
Dieppe 39
Dietz, Howard 162
Dollar Princess, The 160
DOMUM GALOP (Winchester) 109, *110*
Don, Sir William 146

212

Dorset, Duke of 13
Douglas, Christopher 161
DOWN WENT THE WICKET (Colborn) 72, 73
Doyle, Arthur Conan 95
du Terreaux, 106
Duckworth, George 164
Duff, R.A. 70
Duke & Co. 121
Dumas, Felix 48
Dunville, T.E. 155, *156*, 157
Durham 42

Eastman, G.F. 93
EASY COME EASY GO 59
Edgbaston C.C. 135
Edmunds, J. 157, 159
Edocin, Willie 148
Egberts, Bros. 157
Egypt 185
Ellis, F.B. 118
END OF THE SEASON, THE (Timperley) 95
English Game of Cricket, The 41
Englishmen Abroad, The 161
Esmond, Georgie 148
Essex 92-3, 184
ETON AND WINCHESTER (Warner) *111-17*
Eton College 26, *111-17*, 118-21, 125, 132, 134
ETON v. HARROW VALSE *119*
Ettling, Emile 56
Evans, Rev. William A.W. 107
Evans, W. 157
Evans, G.E. 67
EVENING SONG (Box) 41
EVERY DAY IS RAINBOW DAY FOR ME (Lumsdaine) *88*, 89

Fairfax, A. 86
Falkner, Sir Keith 76
FAMOUS BATTEL OF TRENT BRIDGE, YE 141
Faning, Eaton 125, 127
Farjeon, Herbert 162
Farjeon, Jefferson 76
Farjeon Reviewed 162
Farmer, John 121, *122-3*, 125, 127
Farmer, The 135
Favill Press 76
Fawcett, Charles S. 148
Felix on the Bat 39
Fender, Percy 160
Fenner, 137

Fennex, *80*
Fielder, A. 68, 70
FILL THE CUP PHILIP (Warlock) 85
First Test, The 173
Fitzball, E. 139
Fitzgerald 183
Flockton, William 49
FLOORS CASTLE CRICKETERS' SONG (Swain) 42
Fontainbleau, or our Way in France 135
Foster, Basil 160
Foster, R.E. 68
Fourth Stump, The 164
Frampton, Fred 150, *152*
Frindall, Bill 174
Fry, C.B. 63, 70, 105, 151

Gale, F. 54
Gale, Norman 60, 62
Gallatly, James M. 105
Gamble, George 148
Gamble, 20
Garner, Joel 171
Garrett, T.W. 31, 64, *65*
Garrick, David 12
Garth, 23
GENTLEMAN'S A-BOWLING (Harrow) 125
Germany 94
Gibbs, Armstrong 76
Gibbs, L.R. 170
Gifford, Harry 74
Gilbert & Sullivan 107, 146-7, 162
Giles, C.T. 118
Gimblett, Harold 92-4
Glen & Co., W.H. *65*
Glenister, F. 157
Gloucestershire 64
Glover, C. Gordon 164
Goddard, T.W. 168
Gomez, G.E. 168
GOOD OLD HAS-BEENS, THE (Boullemier) 76-7
Goodwill, Kenneth 146
Gover, Alf 163-4
Goward, Annie 148
Grace, Fred 176
Grace, W.G. 17, 31, 44, 46, 50, 64, 73, 95, *101*, 105, 149, 151
Grange, A. Demain 95
Graveney, Tom 164
Graves, A.P. 55, 178
Graves, Maud 148

Graves, Perceval 178
Great Melton, Norfolk 21
Great Ruby, The 149
GREEN GREEN FIELDS 180-1
Greenbank, Percy 160
Greenidge, Gordon 171
Greenock West End C.C. 42
Gregory, David 64, *65*
Greig, Tony 170, 173-4
Grey, Clifford 160
Griffith, *144*
Griffith, C.C. 170
Griffiths, Fred 157
Grimmett, C.V. 86
Grimston, Hon. Robert 121, *122-3*
Grundy, James 141

Haileybury 106
Hales, Walter 148
Halfin, Bob 164
Hall, Frank 56
Hall, W.W. 170
Hambledon 12-14, 79-85, 135, 164
Hammond, Walter 162
Hampshire 12, 14, 63, 135, 166
Hampshire Eskimoes, The *80*, 85
Handsworth C.C. 135
Harding Collection 60
HAROLD GIMBLETT'S HUNDRED 92-4
Harper, Roy 185-6
Harris, Richard 162
Harris, Rolf 165, 173
Harrow 62, 118, 120-5, 166
Hart & Co. 72
Hartopp 138
Hartshead C.C. 42
Hat-Trick, The 162
Hatton, Charles 164
Haverford College, U.S.A. 145
Haworth, Leslie 179
Hawtrey, W.F. 148
Hayes, E. 157, 159
Haynes, Des 171
Hayward, T.W. 68-9
Hearne, *143-4*, 151
Heir at Law 134
HENLEY BOATING MEN'S CHORUS, THE (Risque) 66
HERE'S TO LASCELLES HALL (Lodge) 42
Heriot, W. 148
Hertfordshire *82*
Hewett, H.T. 55

Heywood, Percy 164
HIGH CATCH, THE (Arlott) 176
Hirst, G.H. 68, 70
Hobbs, Jack 90, *91*
Holding, M.A. 171
Hole, Rev. Samuel Reynolds 26-7
Hollywood C.C., U.S.A. 159
Holst, Matthias *16*, *17*
Honey, George 141
HONORARY COLONEL'S SONG, THE (Sullivan) 146
Hookes, D.W. 184
Horan, Thomas 64, *65*
Hornby, Albert Neilson 44
Hornibrook, P.M. 86
Hove 50, *51*, 52
How to Play Clarke 27
HOW'S THAT? (David) 155, *156*
HOW'S THAT? - WELL CAUGHT! 154
Huddesford, George 12
Hughes, Donald 164
Humour of the Age 131
Hurwood, A. 86
Hutt, Bob 157, 159
Hutton, Sir Len 169

I DO LIKE TO BE BESIDE THE SEASIDE 149
I WANT A GIRL (von Tilzer) 73
I Zingari C.C. 28-33, 118, 136
I ZINGARI GALOP (Brosang) *29*
I Zingari *and see* Zingari
I'M RATHER TOO OLD FOR IT NOW 150
Iddison, R. *143-4*
IF TIME IS UP (Bowen) 127
Illingworth, Ray 183
Ilton, Shirley 155, *156*
India 78, 89, 184
Indispensable Rabbit, An 164
Ingle, R.A. 93
Insole, Doug 163
Invalids, The 74, 85
Ireland 23, 135
Irving, Harold 164

Jackson, A. 86
Jackson, F. Stanley ('Jacker') 62, 125
Jackson, John 140
Jagger and the Magical Bat 164
James, Clive 173

Jardine, D.R. 160
JASMINE, THE (Porbandar) 90
Jenkins, 168
Jephson, D.L.A. 54
Jessop, G.L. 160

JOHN BROWN'S BODY 94
Johnson, 141
Johnson over Jordan 162
Johnston, Brian 164, 173-4
JOLLY DOGS 59
Jones, J.G. 109, *110*
JOSSERS' CRICKET CLUB, THE 149

Kallicharan, A.I. 171
Kelly, F.S. *111-17*, 118
Kelvey, W.F. 103
Kenney, J. 135
Kent, 12, 18-19, *82*, 118, 130, 132, 134, 136-7, 184
Kettleband, 20
Key, K.J. 55, 151
King, Collis 171
King, 168
Kingsland, D. 157, 159
Kingston, J.P. 58
Kippax, A.F. 86
Kitchen Laurence 164
Knight, A.E. 68, 71
Knight, 151
Knott, Alan 173
Knox, N.A. 160
Kohler, R.W. 56

Lambert, William 25
Lancashire 44, 178-9, 184
Lambelet, Napoleon 66
Larwood, H. 86, 160-1
Lascelles Hall C.C. 42
Lawrance, Alf J. 74
Lawrence, *143-4*
Laws of Cricket 25, 41
LAWYERS OUT OF MISCHIEF 23
Leeds Theatre *133*
Leer, 'Little' George 14
Lees, Frank & Jack 93
Lees, W. 159
Leicester C.C. 19-21
Leigh, Walter 162
Leno, Dan 157, *158*, 159
Leo, Frank *153*, 154
Lewes, Sussex 25
Lewis, Tony 184-5
Lewis, Vic 183
Leyland, M. 162
LIFE IS LIKE A GAME OF CRICKET (Hall) 56, *57*
LILIAN THOMSON (Stilgoe) 172
Lillee, D.K. 174, 184
Lilley, A.F.A. 68-9
Lillywhite, Fred 137, *142-4*
Lindwall, R. 163
LITTLE BOXES (Seeger) 175
Lloyd, Clive 170
Lockwood, W. 55, 151, 157, 159
Lockyer, Tom *143*
Lodge, E.A. 42
Lohmann, G.A. 55
Long, R.P. 28
Lord's cricket ground 18, 28, 31, 39, 54, 59, *61*, 72, 89, 95, 105, 118, 121, 125, 135, 146, 149, 159, 163, 166-9
Lord's Taverners 163
Love, James 132, 134
Low, Reg 162
Lucas, E.V. 63
Luckes, W.T. 93
Lumsdaine, Jack *87-8*, 89
Lutz, Meyer 41
Lyon, 68
Lyon & Hall, Messrs. 50, *51*, 52
Lyttleton, Edward & Spencer 184
Lyttleton, Hon. R.H. 118

M.C.C. 12, 26, 28, *40*, 72, 135, 161, 163-4, 167, 169, 183-4
McCabe, S. 86
Macfarren, George Alexander 139
Maclagan, T. 59-60, *61*
Maclaren, 'Archie' 66
McNaughton, F. 157
McNaughton, T. 157
Macneice, Louis 164
Maiden Over 164
Manea C.C. 15
Manheim Club, U.S.A. 145
Marlborough College 106
MARRIED v. SINGLE (Sullivan) 146
Marsden, Tom 19-21
Marsh, R.W. 184
Marshall, Malcolm 171
Marshall, *143-4*
Martin, Jack 163
Martineau, Gerard Durani 79
Matheson, Greville E. 105
Mathews, Francis 162
Merchant Taylors School 132
Merion Club, U.S.A. 145

214

Meyder, Karl 32
Middlesex 54-5, 118, 166, 185
MIDNIGHT DREAM (Porbandar) 90
Midwinter, William 64, *65*
Miller, *144*
Millhillians, Old 166
Mills, H.G.L. 49
Mills, J.D. 41-2
Monckton, Lionel 160
Monro, Harold 76
MOONLIGHT RIPPLES (Porbandar) 90
Moorat, Joseph 60, 62
More Songs and Snatches 178
Morell, H.H. 66
Mortimer, Amy & A.E. 63
Mortlock, W. *143-4*
Morton, Thomas 135
Moss, F.W. 157
Mott, W. 159
Mouillot, Frederick 66
Moule, Ken 162
Mudie, W. *143-4*
Murdoch, William 64, *65*
Murray, D. 170-1
Murray-Lane, Henry 94
MY CRICKET GIRL (Leo) 151, *153*
MY FRIENDS LEAVE YOUR WORK NOW TO SPORT AND TO PLAY 24
Mynn, Alfred 137

Nainby, R. 148
Napier, Russell 162
NATURAL HISTORY MATCH IN THREE INNINGS, A (Gifford) 74
Nayudu, C.K. 89
Nelson, Daniel H.C. 21
New Zealand 64, 78
Newmarket 132, 134
Nicholls, 55
Nichols ('Maurice Nick') 93-4
NOBLE GAME OF CRICKET, THE 12
Northamptonshire C.C.C. 58
Norwich 131
Nottingham 19-21, 55, 139-41
Novello, Vincent 13
Novello & Co. 120, 139
Nyren, John 13-14, *83*

O.B.s BATTLE-SONG (Old Broughtonians) *75*, 76
O'Connor, J. 93
O'Donnell, B.W. 76

O'Gorman brothers 184
O'Keeffe, John 135
O'Nester, Alf 157
Odiham C.C. 14
Ogston, Bruce 181
OH THE SHEFFIELDERS 42
OLD BOYS' MATCH, THE (Uppingham) 109
OLD ENGLISH CRICKETER, THE 26
OLD-FASHIONED LOCKET 89
Old Trafford 179
Oldfield, W.A. 86
Olympian C.C. 163
ON SURREY HILLS (Banstead) 106
One Eye Wild 164
ORIENTAL ENSEMBLE, AN (Porbandar) 90
ORIENTAL MOON (Porbandar) 90
Oscroft, 140
Ossett C.C. 42
OUR BUNGALOW OF DREAMS 89
OUR DON BRADMAN 89
OUR ELEVEN (Lumsdaine) 86, *87*
Our Miss Gibbs 160
OUT 150
Outside Edge 162
Oval 54, 59, *61*, 142, *144*, 157, *158*, 176,
Oxford 26, 60, 107, 118, 121, 132

Packer, Kerry 173-4, 184
Pagliarin, Marie 90
Paine, Ralph D. 145
Pakistan 185
Panther Larkin 164
Park, G. 159
Parr, Frank 184
Parr, George 141
Parry, Derek 171
Pascoe, Len 184
Patel, Bachu 163
Patterson, William Seeds 109
Paul, Howard 59
PEACE, PEACE (Monckton) 160
Pearce, T.N. 93
Pearman, J. & W. 59, *61*
Percival, Robert 42
Perkins, Theron D. *30*
Perman, Percy 157
Perman, Willie 157

Petersfield 13
Philaster 133, 134
Phydora, C. 157, 159
Phyllis at the wicket 179
Pilch, Fuller 59, *61*, 137
Plairre, Charles 147
Plater, Alan 162
Playford, Henry 11
Poluskis, Bros. 157
Pond, C. *143-4*
Ponsford, W.M. 86
Ponsonby, Hon. F. 28, 121, *122-3*, 136
Ponsonby-Fane, Sir Spencer 28
Poor Gentleman, The 134, 136
Porbandar, Maharaja of 89-90
Porter, A.D. 33
Porter, Samuel 19
Pratt, Charles E. *65*
Preston-Thomas, H. 28
Priestley, J.B. 162
PRIMROSE AND BLUE, THE 146
protest songs 179-82
Purcell, Henry 11

RADNAGE CRICKET SONG, THE 14
Rae, A.F. 168
Ramadhin, S. 168
Randall, D.W. 173-4
Randegger, Alberto 106
RANJI (West) 50, *51*
Ranjitsinhji, K.S. 50-4, 149
RANJITSINHJI WALTZ (West) 52, *53*
Rape of Helen, The 131
Rashid, Haroon 185
RASPBERRY TIME IN RUNCORN (Coward) 130
Rattigan, Terence 162
Raven, Simon 164
Rawlins, 19
Read, W.W. 31, 55, 151
REBECCA OF SUNNYBROOK FARM 161
RED IS RED AND BLUE IS BLUE 172
Reeder & Walsh *156*
Reimers, Christian 108
Relf, A.E. 68, 70
RHAPSODY (Butterworth) 118
Rhodes, W. 68, 70
Rice, Tim 5-7, 173
Richards, Viv 171
Richardson, V.Y. 86
Richmond Heiress; or a Woman

once in the Right, The 131
Richter, W. 109
RIGHT CRICKETER, THE (Mortimer) 63-4
Risque, W.H. 66, 159
Roberts, Aldwyn (Lord Kitchener) 169-70
Roberts, A.M.E. 171
Robinson, Percy S. 90, *91*, 163
ROEDEAN XI *128-9*
ROLL ON THE COVERS 165
Rollit, George 159
Roman Catholic cricketers 56
Ross, Adrian 160
Rossall School XI 185
ROUND-HAND BOWLING (du Terreaux) 106
Rowe, Lawrence 171
RUB IT IN (Gale) 60
Rubens, Paul 160

Sager, Alf 157
St. Claire, Edward 79
Sangeet Mela 163
Sargent, E. ('Tanny') 145
Sartin, Bonny 177
Sassoon, Siegfried 95
Scarborough 56, 118
'Schism of 1866' 139-41
SCHOOL CRICKET SONG, THE (Wakefield) 103-4
school songs 96-129, 132
Schwartz, Arthur 162
Scotland 42
Scott-Gatty, A. *35-8*
Sedbergh school 96, *97-102*
Sedgwick, Laura 148
SEE THE CRICKETERS OF KENT (Porter) 18-19
Seeger, Pete 175
SERGEANT'S SONG, THE (Sullivan) 146
Sewell, *143-4*
Shakespeare, William 130
Sharif, Omar 185
Shaw, Alfred 140, 176
Shaw, J.C. 140
SHE DIDN'T KNOW ENOUGH ABOUT THE GAME (Rollit) 159
She Stoops to Conquer 139
Sheffield C.C. 19-21, 42
Sherriff, R.C. 161
Shrewsbury School 107
SHROPSHIRE LAD, A (Butterworth) 118

Shuter, J. 55
Simon Says 162
Sims, Albert 148
SING A SONG OF CRICKETERS (Timperley) 95-6
SING MUSE THE MAN, 24, 25
Six Balls Out 164
Sixty Years of Uppingham Cricket 109
SLOWMAN'S CHANT 26
Small family 13, *83*
Smith, Bruce 157
Smith, C. Aubrey, 159, 183
Smith, J. Harcourt 44, *45*
Smith, Peter 93
Smith, Ray 93
Smith, William 132, 134
Snaith, J.C. 76
SNAKE-CHARMER, THE (Porbandar) 90
Snow, John 174, 185-6
SNOW IN THE WEST INDIES (Stilgoe) 174
Sobers, Sir Gary 170
SOLDIERS OF THE WILLOW (Evans) *67*
Sofaer, Abraham 162
Somerset, 55, 92-4, 171, 178
SONG OF CRICKET, A (Behrend) 54
SONG OF THE CRICKETER, THE (Lutz) 41
SONG OF THE CRICKETER, THE (Thirlwall) 41
SONG OF THE EMERITI, THE (Welman) 56
SONG OF THE ENGLISH CRICKETERS (Lyon) 68-71
SONG OF THE FAST BOWLER, A 183
SONG OF THE GAMES (Wycombe) 127
SONGS OF THE BAT (Lucas) 63
SPARKLING (Gale) 62
Speed the Plough 135
Spencer, Don 165
Spiers, F. *143*
Spofforth, F.R. 31, 64, *65*
Sporting Songs 27
Sportive Snatches 147-9
Squire, Sir John 74
Squire, J.C. 79
Staincliffe C.C. 42

Staples, R. Ponsonby 31
Stebb, 157
Stedman, F. 159
Stephenson, Edward *143-4*
Stephenson, H.H. *144*
Stevens, George Alexander 131
Sticky Wicket 164
STICKY WICKET BLUES (Adams) 174-5
Stilgoe, Richard 172-4
Stollmeyer, Jeffrey 168-9
Straus, Ralph 76
Strudwick, H. 68, 71
Stuart, Leslie 159
Sueter, Tom 14, *80*
SUNSHINE (Haworth) 179
Surrey 21, 25, 54-5, 69, 79, 139-41, *142-4*, 160, 184
Sussex 50, 52, 70, 72, 79, 92, 137-8
SUSSEX WELCOME TO THE WANDERER, A 52
Sutch, Henry A. 47
Sutherland, Joan 173
Sutton, Kent 49
Swain, W. 42
Swanton, E.W. 173
Sydney, Harry *142-4*
Sylvester Music Co. Ltd. *91*
SYMPHONY OF THE TREES (Porbandar) 90

Tales from the Long Room 164
Tanner, James T. 66
Tate, H. 157
Tate, Maurice 164
Tatem, 157
Taunton 55-6, 92
TAVERNERS SONG, THE (Robinson) 163
Taylor, Alfred D. 72
Taylor, Charles 137-8
Taylor, Tom 136
Taylor, *82*
Teignbridge C.C. 26
television and radio 18, 90, 163-7, 173-4, 176-7
Test Matches 18, 64, 66, 68, 86, 89, 92, 149, 161, 167-74
THAT'S NOT CRICKET 162
theatre and music hall 128-63
Thirlwall, J.W. *40*, 41
Thomas, P.A. 96
Thoms, 54
Thomson, Frank 46
Thomson, Jeff 172
Thorne, Ken 183

Thorns, Francis 105
Thornton, Charles Inglis 118
Thorpe, Charles 58
Thring, Rev. Edward 108
TIE MATCH, THE 42
Tilling, 144
Time and Time Again 162
Timperley, H.W. 95
Tinley, Chris 140
Tinniswood, Peter 164
TONBRIDGE SCHOOL CRICKET SONG 107-8
Too Many Cooks 135
touring songs 182-4
Travers, Ben 161
TREATS OF LONDON, THE 135
Tremmer, G. 159
Trentham C.C. 76
Trepp, 157
Tressider, A. 157
Trevor, Harry & Leo 34-8
Trott, A.E. 151
Trueman, Fred 172
Tunbridge Wells 94
Turner, F. 159
TWO HUNDRED YEARS OF CRICKET (Stilgoe) 173-4
Tyldesley, J.T. 68-9
Tyler, E.J. 55

United States of America *30*, 64, 145-6, 162
UP AT LORD'S (Matheson) 105-6
Upgreen - and at 'em or A Maiden Nearly over 163
Uppingham School 108-9
Utopia Ltd. 147

Valentine, A.L. 168
VALSE I ZINGARI (Porter) *33*
Verga, E. 90
VETERAN'S SONG, THE (Sullivan) 146
VEXED BOWLER, THE 41
Vicat, Alice 148
Victoria C.C. 135

VILLAGE CRICKET 165-6
VILLAGE RONDO, THE (Holst) 16, 17
Vincent, 19
Vocal Cabinet (Armiger) 21
Von Tilzer, Harry 73

Wade, T.H. 93
Wakefield Northern Congregational School 103
Walcott, C.L. 168
Walderton Common, Sussex 18
Wales 108, 180-1, 184-5
Walker, C. 86
Walker, family *144*
Walker London 149
Wall, T.M. 86
Walton, Sam 73
Wanostrocht, Nicholas ('Felix') 21, 27, 39, 41
Ward, William 28
Wardle, J.H. 168
Warlock, Peter 79, *80-4*, 85
Warner, P.F. 68
Warner, R.T. *111-17*, 118
Warner, 149
Warton, Major 183
Washbrook, C. 169
Waugh, Alec 76
Watling, Peter 162
WE GOT THOMMO 172
Weekes & Co. 49, 52, *53*, 105
Weippert & Co. 59, *61*
Wellard, Arthur 93
Wellington, Duke of 41, 96
Wells, G. *144*
Welman, C. 56
Welsh, 157
West, Charles T. 50, *51*, 52,*53*, 54
West Indies 163, 167-72, 174
Whalley-Tooker, E. 79
WHAT'S A POMMIE (Spencer) 165
WHEN AN OLD CRICKETER LEAVES THE CREASE (Harper) 185-6
When the Meadows are aglow 179
WHEN THIS BLOODY

TOUR IS OVER 184
White, Jack 92
White, Jean *30*
White, J.C. 93
Whitty, May 148
WHO WERE YOU WITH LAST NIGHT 149
WHO'S GROVELLING NOW (Gray) 170
Wilderness of Monkeys 162
Williams, Joseph 106
Willis, Grinnell 145
WILLOW THE KING (Harrow) 121, *122-4*
Wilson, David Henry 170
Winchester, 12, 109, *110-17*, 118
Winslow Boy, The 162
Wit and Mirth: Or Pills to Purge Melancholy 11, 131
WONDERFUL JOY OUR EYES TO BLESS, A (Sullivan) 147
Wood, P.J. 103
Woodfull, W.M. 86
Woods, Sammy 55
Wootton, G. 141
Worcestershire 68, 70, 160
World of Cricket, The 90
Wright, Julian 95
Wyatt, R.E.S. 164
Wycombe School 127
Wynne, Ellis J. 60, 62
Wynnewood Ground, U.S.A. 145

Yardley, N. 168
Yorkshire 62, 69-70, 139, *143-4*, 179

Zelman, Alberto *67*
ZINGARI GALOP (Meyder) *32*
ZINGARI MARCH TWO STEP (Perkins) *30*
Zingari *and see* I Zingari
'ZUMBADI' CONCERTO, THE (Porbandar) 90
ZUMMERZET VARSUS ZURREY (Graves) 55, 178

INDEX OF FIRST LINES

A bunch of the boys went sailing away 86
A tickle o' me spinnin' finger 177
And now, my boys, give one cheer more 23
And now the game is ended, boys 14
As Cricketers all know the feeling 143
Assist all ye muses, and join to rehearse 12
At cricket, her kin will lose or win 147
Attend all ye Muses 12

Bicknoller was his village, Harold Gimblett was his name 92-4
But the summer term is best, for we're out from morn till night 127
But who are these array'd in white with bat and ball and wicket? 66

Come all, great, small, short, tall, away to Stoolball 11
Come listen all good people 138-9
Cricket, lovely cricket 168-9

De West Indians have come to town 170-2
Durham City has been dull so long 42

England was in trouble from the very start 170
Ev'ry morning on the radio, the news comes to Australia 172-3
Ev'ry time we play our game 183
For Euphony's sake it were p'rhaps quite as well 21

Get yer coat, get yer hat 178
Glorious sounds are the whish and the whack 145
Good evening, friends! Of course you all know me 149

He may have been little, or may have been tall 126
Her (he) was the Prettiest fellow 12, 131
His score became history, at the local thatched inn 163
Hurrah for the days of victory 56
Hurrah, Hurrah, for the noble game of cricket 139

I got the blues - my baby's bereft me 174-5
I like a game of billiards upon the cloth so green 49
I read the Daily Telegraph's account of Doctor Grace 46
I sing a glorious hero bold, his name well known to fame 50
I was watching Middlesex and Hampshire play at Lord's 166-7
If time is up and lesson is due, and youth has got to learn 127

If you've England in your veins 98-102
I'll make a song of Hambledon, and sing it at 'The George' *80-4*
I'm not a good Cover I freely admit 62
In a cricket match I was picked to play 155, *156*
In Canada they have la crosse 49
In Melbourne on the Ides of March in 1877 174
In seventeen hundred and ninety-one 15
It's another tale of love altho' it's not about a loon 151

Jolly Sun, we do implore thee 109

Last night I lay a-dreaming, I was batting up at Lord's 105-6
Let others hunt, or fish, or sail 60
Lillee pounds them down like a machine 184
Listen! There's a murmur in the downland 78
Listen well to our song, it's not a time for mirth 181-2
Little boxes in the sports shop 175
Long, long on lawn of noble 27

Mister Cricket ev'ry ev'ning sat 74

No Spanish Don with a long pedigree 62
Now it's never been the same 180-1
Now this new kind of cricket takes courage to stick it 161
Now you teach a girl to ride a bike and she runs into a wall 150

O cabby trot him faster 125
O' the cricket 1st XI 128, *129*
Of all the games in Scotland, good cricket is the best 42
Of all the Joys our Parents did Partake 132
Oh, Ranji is it you dear 52
Oh! the steamship 'Orontes' arrived in the bay 68-71
Old England's great boast I propose as a toast 35-8
Once I thought I'd like to be a cricketer 154
Patiently our favourite plays 54-5
Pilch, Lillywhite, and Fenner - I declare! 137-8
Play the grand old game once more 67

'Rugger' is grand on a winter's day 95

See the cricketers of Kent 18-19
Sing a song of Cricketers 96

That I was one of the M.C.C. 164-5
The cricket is a jolly elf 145
The cricketer laid his bat aside 64

218

The feast it is over, let wine cups be spread 59
The field's the world in which we wage 56
The Lawyers went in and the first case was called on 23
The M.C.C. proclaim that they are not pleased 169
The Marylebone ranks first of all 28
The season has started and cricket is here 165
The stranger hit that mighty skier 176
Then when our game is over 58
There's an Animal Test Match at Sunnybrook Farm 161
There's the Opera House at the West 135
They tell of Brown of Brighton 17-18
Though Itchen flows apart from Thames 112-17
Though the Muses be silent and History's pages 120
To cricket we call you, to dare and to do 107-8
To live a life, free from gout, pain or phthisic 21
Toss him down a slow you see 62-3

Unless you possess a cricketer's guide *144*
Up North when we play the Yorkshire tykes 179

You may boast of the pleasures untold 49

You may laugh if you like, but such is the case 72
We all arrived in Bath one day at Clifford Bax's 75
We are the good old Has-beens 76-7
We are told England's armies assembled 31
We love to roam away from home 146
Well, o'course we cheered vor Zummerzet as long 55
West Indies and England met once again 169
We've got the Ashes back home 183
What means this paper warfare and these spites 140-1
What's the matter, my friends, at Sheffield to-day 19-20
When a copper's not engaged in playing cricket 147
When last we met, who would have thought 22
When it's raspberry time in Runcorn 130
When quite a lad I always loved 73
When the last day is done 186
When you've buckled on your pads to wield the willow 103-4
Who is it that all Australia raves about? 89
Will, Tom, Hall, Dick and Hugh 11
Willow the king is a monarch grand *123-4*
With a bat and a ball and a wicket 160